Essential Series

Springer-Verlag London Ltd.

Also in this series:

John Vince
Essential Virtual Reality *fast*
1-85233-012-0

John Cowell
Essential Visual J++ 6.0 *fast*
1-85233-013-9

John Cowell
Essential Java 2 *fast*
1-85233-071-6

John Cowell
Essential Visual Basic 6.0 *fast*
1-85233-071-6

John Vince
Essential Computer Animation *fast*
1-85233-141-0

Aladdin Ayesh
Essential Dynamic HTML *fast*
1-85233-626-9

David Thew
Essential Access 2000 *fast*
1-85233-295-6

Ian Palmer
Essential Java 3D *fast*
1-85233-394-4

Matthew Norman
Essential ColdFusion *fast*
1-85233-315-4

Ian Chivers
Essential Linux *fast*
1-85233-408-8

Fiaz Hussain
Essential Flash 5.0 *fast*
1-85233-451-7

John Vince
Essential Mathematics for
Computer Graphics *fast*
1-85233-380-4

John Cowell
Essential VB .NET *fast*
1-85233-591-2

Simon Stobart
Essential PHP *fast*
1-85233-578-5

Fiaz Hussain
Essential Dreamweaver 4.0 *fast*
1-85233-573-4

Aladdin Ayesh
Essential UML *fast*
1-85233-413-4

Ian Stephenson
Essential RenderMan *fast*
1-85233-608-0

Dan Lavender
Essential Maya 4 *fast*
1-85233-588-2

Simon Stobart

Essential
ASP.NET™
fast

with examples in VB .NET

 Springer

Simon Stobart, BA(Hons), Ph.D, MBCS, CEng
School of Computing and Technology, University of Sunderland,
Sunderland SR6 0DD

Series Editor
John Cowell, BSc (Hons), MPhil, PhD
Department of Computer Science, De Montfort University, The Gateway,
Leicester LE1 9BH

British Library Cataloguing in Publication Data
Stobart, Simon
    Essential ASP.NET fast : with examples in VB .NET. – (Essential
    series)
    1. Active Server Pages (Computer file)   2. Internet
    programming   3. ASP.NET fast
    005.2'76
ISBN 978-1-85233-683-7   ISBN 978-1-4471-0005-8 (eBook)
DOI 10.1007/978-1-4471-0005-8

Library of Congress Cataloging-in-Publication Data
A catalog record for this book is available from the Library of Congress

Essential series ISSN 1439-975X

ISBN 978-1-85233-683-7

http://www.springer.co.uk

© Springer-Verlag London 2003
Originally published by Springer-Verlag London Berlin Heidelberg in 1997

Typesetting: electronic text files prepared by the author

34/3830-543210

Contents

Chapter 1

Why Use ASP.NET?

Introduction

ASP.NET is a technology developed by Microsoft to enable you to create dynamic web applications. ASP.NET is part of the .NET framework which also includes VB.NET, C++.NET, C#.NET among others.

If you are wishing to create web enabled applications and/or link new or existing databases to the Web then you are going to need to be able to program in a dynamic web language. There are a number of alternative technologies for doing this but ASP.NET is one of the latest means of accomplishing this.

Before you begin ASP.NET development you must at first decide which programming language you are going to use. What, do I have a choice? I hear you say. Well, yes you certainly do, as the .NET framework has been designed to allow third party companies to plug in their own languages into the framework. Currently, the .NET framework comes with C#, C++ and VB.NET as standard.

What about ASP? ASP is a previous Microsoft dynamic web language, which has been superseded by ASP.NET. ASP syntax was based around a cut-down version of Visual Basic. As Microsoft expects most ASP developers to migrate to the new ASP.NET environment we have chosen to use VB.NET as the language of choice in our examples throughout this book.

What do I need?

In order to begin ASP.NET development you will need four things:

• A fairly new PC with a reasonably fast processor.

- An operating system, which supports the Internet Information Server (IIS). Currently such operating systems include Windows .NET Server, Windows NT 4.0, Windows 2000 and Windows XP.
- The Internet Information Server
- The .NET framework

The Internet Information Server comes as standard with Windows .NET Server, Windows NT 4.0, Windows 2000 and Windows XP. However, it is not necessarily installed by default with Windows 2000 and Windows XP and so you will need to install this yourself.

The .NET framework is available free of charge from the Microsoft web site. In Chapter 2 we shall examine how to install both of these products.

Is this book for you?

This book does assume that you are familiar with using the Windows operating system and some of its applications such as spreadsheets and word processors. It also assumes that you have some prior experience in using programming languages and in particular Visual Basic. While a brief summary of the Visual Basic .NET programming language is included in Chapter 4 you may find that reading Essential VB.NET *fast*, also part of the Essential Series, is worthwhile if you are unfamiliar with this language.

If you have experience of developing in ASP you may feel that you are going to have a bit of a head start over someone who does not. However, this book does not make any assumptions that you have had such experience of using this language. In fact there are some quite substantial differences between ASP and ASP.NET, something that the experienced ASP developer will need to bear in mind.

This book is not a complete reference text. We simply do not have enough pages to describe every feature and aspect of the ASP.NET language. We do however cover quite a large range of the features and functions of the language and provide the necessary knowledge so that you will be capable of creating your own database enabled dynamic web sites.

If you don't have the time to read a 1000+ page book on ASP.NET development then you will find that Essential ASP.NET is a good introduction to web based development using VB.NET.

How to use this book

This book contains many examples and screen shots to help you understand the concepts and ideas it introduces. It is structured into chapters that will lead you through the basics of ASP.NET application development.

The book should normally be read from start to finish, but each chapter can be read in isolation once you are familiar with the basics of the VB.NET language.

Chapter 2 describes how to install and configure an ASP.NET development environment.

Chapter 3 introduces the ASP.NET environment and explains how to begin to develop ASP.NET applications.

Chapter 4 describes the basics of the VB.NET language, including variables and functions, string handling, expressions, operators, operands, flow of control, functions and subroutines.

Chapter 5 introduces some ASP.NET objects and describes how they can be used.

Chapter 6 introduces the concept of user interaction and describes how ASP.NET forms can be used to obtain user input.

Chapters 7, 8 and 9 examine ASP.NET web server controls in more detail and describe the different properties, which can be used to enhance their functionality.

Chapter 10 introduces form validation and explains the mechanisms which have been built into ASP.NET to assist the developer.

Chapter 11 looks at file handling and cookies and explains how to create and manipulate them.

Chapters 12 and 13 examine how databases can be linked to ASP.NET applications and be used to produce database enabled dynamic web environments.

Finally, Chapter 14 provides some clues on where to go next for further information and describes some useful web resources.

Don't Type!

All of the program examples in this book are available from the Essential Series web site:

www.Essential-Series.com

so you don't need to type any of the examples if you don't want to.

So, let's get started. The next chapter examines the software needed to begin creating your own ASP.NET applications.

Chapter 2

The ASP.NET Environment

Introduction

This chapter will explain how to configure your compiler in order that you can begin developing ASP.NET applications.

Basic Software Components

There are two main items of software that you need to obtain in order to begin ASP.NET development. These are:

•   The Internet Information Server

•   The .NET framework

You will also need an operating system and personal computer, which supports the Internet Information Server (IIS). Currently such operating systems include Windows .NET Server, Windows NT 4.0, Windows 2000 and Windows XP. We shall assume that you have a PC running one of these operating systems and are ready to obtain the additional software components.

Installing Internet Information Server

The Internet Information Server (IIS) comes as standard with Windows .NET Server, Windows NT 4.0, Windows 2000 and Windows XP. However, it may not be installed by default with Windows 2000 and Windows XP.

To install IIS click the **Start** button, point to **Settings** and click **Control Panel**. A window similar to that shown in Figure 2.1 should appear.

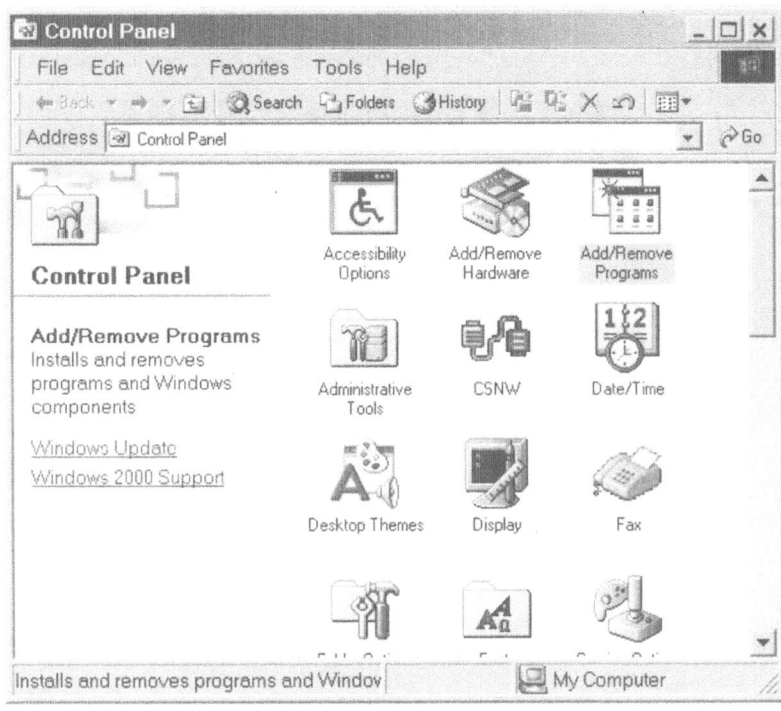

Figure 2.1 Control Panel

You should then select and start the **Add/Remove Programs** application from this menu. From the **Add/Remove Programs** application click the **Add/Remove Windows Components** button, shown in Figure 2.2.

A Windows Components Wizard box should appear, similar to that shown in Figure 2.3. Simply check the **Tickbox** next to the Internet Information Services (IIS) component and click the **Next** button.

Follow the on-screen instructions to install this software.

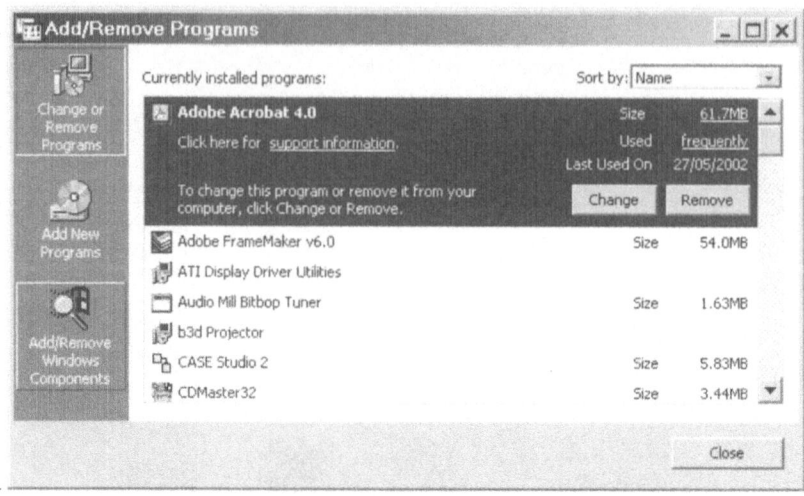

Figure 2.2 Add/Remove Programs application

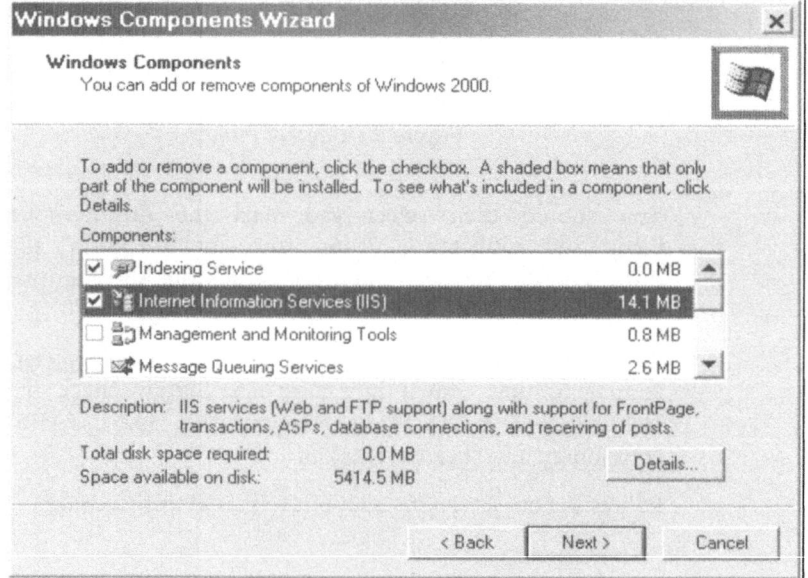

Figure 2.3 Windows Components Wizard

Running Internet Information Server

It is useful to have IIS automatically running whenever your computer is switched on. You can check if the Internet Information Server is running by the presence of the following icon on the Windows toolbar shown in Figure 2.4.

Figure 2.4 IIS Icon

Clicking on this icon launches the **Personal Web Manager**, shown in Figure 2.5, which allows you, amongst other things, to stop and start the IIS.

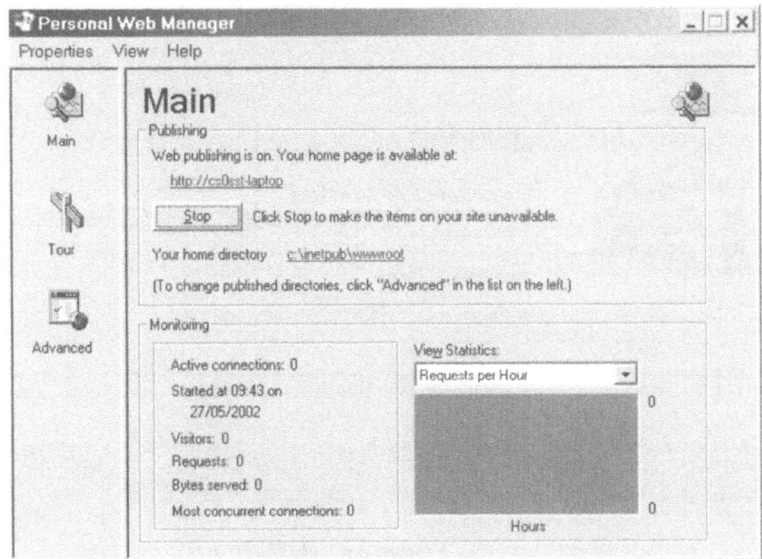

Figure 2.5 Personal Web Manager

Obtaining the .NET Framework

Once you have a working IIS you also need to obtain the .NET framework. This is available free from the Microsoft web site at:

http://msdn.microsoft.com/netframework/downloads/sp1/default.asp

The .NET framework web site is shown in Figure 2.6.

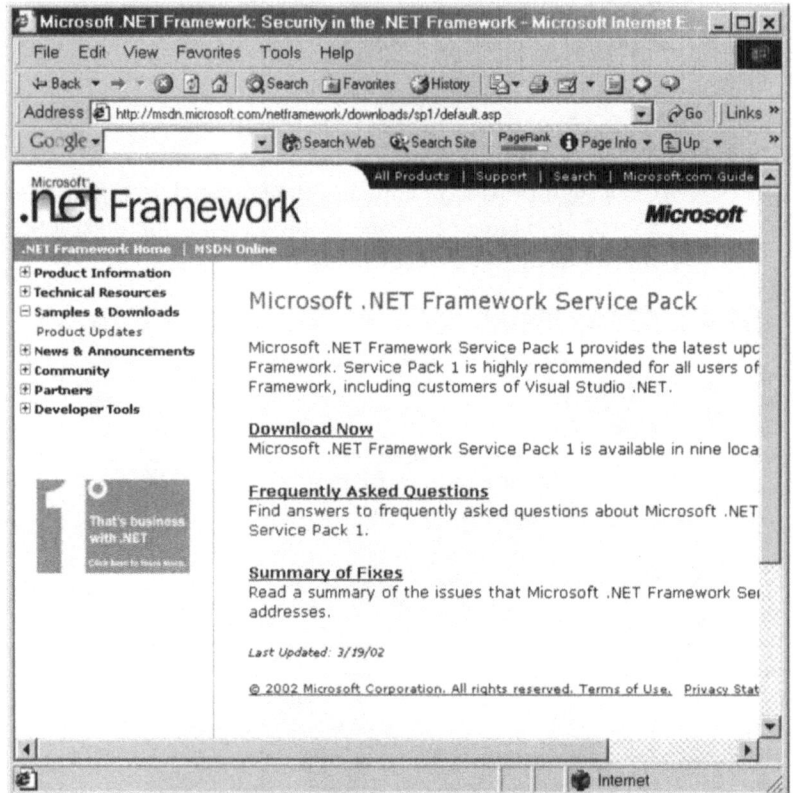

Figure 2.6 .NET web site

You should select the download option, which installs the .NET framework automatically. Once downloaded the .NET framework will automatically detect the presence of the IIS and install accordingly.

Your ASP.NET Development Directory

Having installed your IIS server you should create a directory in which all of your ASP.NET scripts can be saved. Using Windows Explorer access the following directory (or one of your choosing):

C:\Inetpub\wwwroot\

and create a sub-directory called **aspnetbook**:

C:\Inetpub\wwwroot\aspnetbook\

All of the examples in the following chapters should be saved in this directory.

Summary

This chapter has examined how to create an ASP.NET development environment. We are now ready to commence ASP.NET programming and in the next chapter we can introduce our first ASP.NET program.

Chapter

3

Introducing ASP.NET

Introduction

The standard hypertext mark-up language (HTML) was designed as a means to create hypertext documents. It is not a programming language and although it can be used to construct user interface forms allowing a user to interact with a web page, it cannot be used alone to build interactive dynamic computer systems. In order to produce web pages whose content is dynamic, some other technologies are required. One such technology is ASP.NET.

In this chapter we shall examine our first ASP.NET script. We shall examine the basics of ASP.NET, how it works and what it can be used for. We will also introduce some simple ASP.NET statements.

A Simple HTML Document

You should be familiar with the basic elements and syntax of the HTML script shown below:

```html
<html>
    <head>
        <title>chapt3-1.htm Simple HTML Page</title>
    </head>
    <body>
    <h1>Welcome to my Web Page</h1>
    <p>
    This is a simple HTML document which illustrates some of the
    basic HTML elements.</p>
    <p>
    There should be nothing here which is unusual to you.</p>
    </body>
</html>
```

If you wish you can type this script in using your chosen text editor. To check that it works, save it as **chapt3-1.htm** in the following directory of your Microsoft IIS Web Server:

C:\Inetpub\wwwroot\aspnetbook\

You can view this document by typing localhost/aspnetbook/chapt3-1.htm in your browser location window and pressing return. Figure 3.1 illustrates what should be displayed.

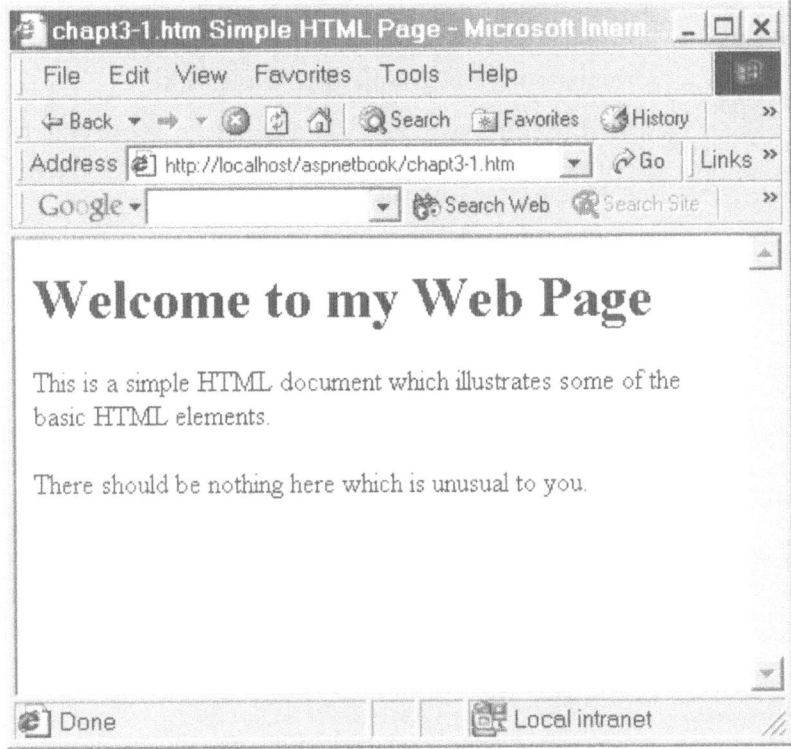

Figure 3.1 *Simple HTML page*

HTML script uses elements and tags to mark up the document. In this simple example the title of the page is defined within the <title> ... </title> tags and the page heading is defined within the <h1> ... </h1> tags.

What is ASP.NET and ASP?

ASP.NET is technology to assist in creating real world web applications. It is not a programming language like Visual Basic or Java that you purchase and install on your computer ready to begin software development. ASP.NET forms part of the Microsoft .NET framework.

The .NET framework provides support for many different programming languages and comes with built in support for the following languages:

• Visual Basic

• C#

• C++

• JScript (a form of JavaScript)

One of the powerful features of ASP.NET programming is that it is very flexible and you are free to choose which of these languages you want to use to develop your ASP.NET applications. In this book we have chosen to use Visual Basic .NET as the language to illustrate the examples, as it is likely to be the most popular choice for implementing ASP.NET applications. ASP.NET pages work with a wide range of web browsers including Netscape, Opera and of course Internet Explorer.

Some of you may have had experience of (or have read about) an earlier scripting language developed by Microsoft in 1996, called ASP. ASP or Active Server Pages provided support for an interpreted VBScript (a cut down version of Visual Basic). ASP allowed you to insert this code alongside the HTML script to form a web page. The ASP code was interpreted each time the page was requested by a web browser and a dynamic web page was created. ASP was very successful, but it was not perfect. ASP.NET has been developed to replace ASP and is quite different in the way it operates. However, like ASP, ASP.NET is a server-side language, which means it is processed at the server not the client browser. Unlike ASP, ASP.NET provides full implementations of programming languages so that it is very powerful. It is a compiled language, which means it is far faster than an interpreted one. The rule here is to be careful when referring to these technologies, as ASP is not the same as ASP.NET.

First ASP.NET Script

As mentioned, ASP.NET is a server-side embedded language. ASP.NET code is inserted into the HTML document and uses tags to denote the start and end of the ASP.NET programming instructions. To explain what this means we had best introduce a simple example:

```
<%@Page Language="VB" Debug="True" %>

<html>
    <head>
    <title>chapt3-2.aspx First Script</title>
    </head>

    <body>
    <% Dim intHeading As Integer %>
    <% For intHeading = 1 To 6 %>
        <h<%=intHeading %>>
        This is Heading size <%=intHeading %>
        </h<%=intHeading %>>
    <% Next %>
    </body>
</html>
```

Don't worry about how this works at the moment – we shall cover these instructions in later chapters. All we wanted to show you was what an ASP.NET script looks like and how one can be created.

This example looks similar to a simple HTML script. However, if you look more closely you will see that there are some new scripting elements in the document. The first element is:

```
<%@Page Language="VB" Debug="True" %>
```

This element is known as the page header and is usually found as the first line of an ASP.NET web document. While it is not required it is good practice to include it. The page header is enclosed with ASP.NET delimiters:

```
<% %>
```

The delimiters mark the start and end of ASP.NET code. Anything inside the delimiters is ASP.NET and outside is standard HTML. The page header consists of a number of page parameter settings. In this example these are:

```
Language="VB"
Debug="True"
```

The first of these, **Language**, specifies which programming language is being used in the page. In this case it is Visual Basic. Visual Basic for ASP.NET applications is known as VB.NET. The second parameter sets the value of **Debug** equal to **"true"**. This ensures that full error messages are created if the compiler finds an error in your page. When you have finished creating your page this parameter can be removed to ensure a performance gain when processing your web pages. All of the examples in this book will however include this setting.

The next few lines of the page are standard HTML:

```
<html>
    <head>
    <title>chapt3-2.aspx First Script</title>
    </head>
    <body>
```

Following these is the line:

```
<% Dim intHeading As Integer %>
```

This is an ASP.NET instruction written in VB.NET and the code appears within the <% and %> delimiters. This line defines a variable called **intHeading** as an integer type. We shall discuss variables in Chapter 4. The next line is an ASP.NET instruction:

```
<% For intHeading = 1 To 6 %>
```

This is the first line of a loop structure. Loops allow the lines of code within them to be executed a number of times. In this case the loop will iterate six times. Loops are discussed is Chapter 4. The next three lines of code are a combination of ASP.NET and standard HTML:

```
<h<%=intHeading %>>
This is Heading size <%=intHeading %>
</h<%=intHeading %>>
```

The <%=intHeading %> instructions are the ASP.NET way of displaying the content of a variable. In this case the value of intHeading. Finally, the last line of ASP.NET code is:

```
<% Next %>
```

This marks the end of the loop. The last two lines of the page are standard HTML:

```
    </body>
</html>
```

You should enter this script in your chosen text editor and save this as chapt3-2.aspx in the following directory of your Microsoft Internet Information Services Web Server:

```
C:\Inetpub\wwwroot\aspnetbook\
```

Note, that all ASP.NET scripts should be saved with the extension ".aspx" to differentiate them from the old .asp files. To access this script type:

```
http://localhost/aspnetbook/chapt3-2.aspx
```

into your browser address window. Figure 3.2 illustrates what should be displayed.

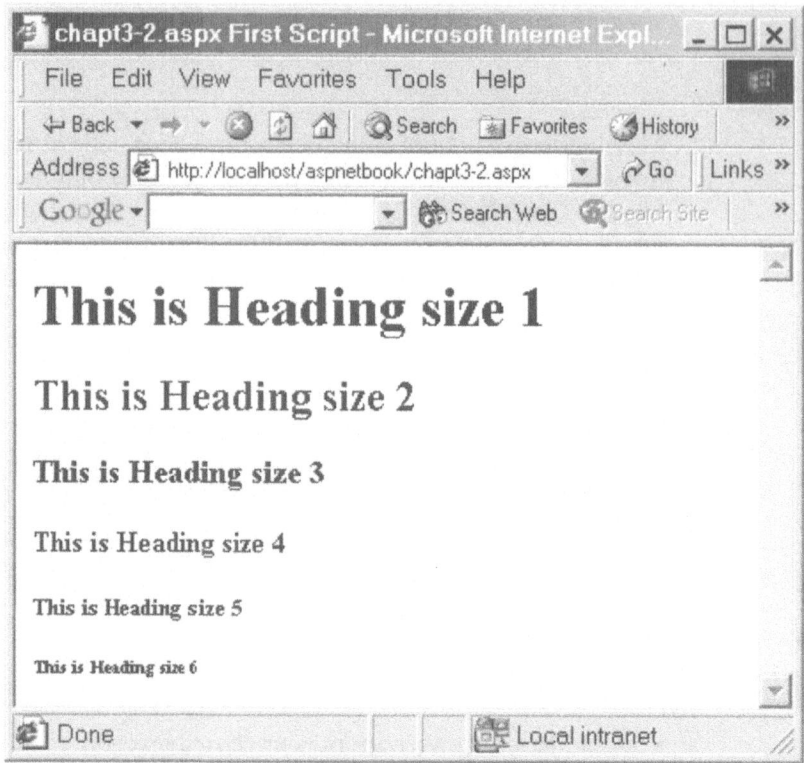

Figure 3.2 Output from our first ASP.NET example

Alternative Script

If all has gone well you will have successfully produced your first ASP.NET page. Don't worry if you don't fully understand it yet, we don't expect you to. Each of these instructions will be examined in later chapters. However, for now take a look at the following code:

```
<html>
    <head>
    <title>chapt3-3.html First Script</title>
```

```
</head>

<body>
        <h1>This is Heading size 1</h1>
        <h2>This is Heading size 2</h2>
        <h3>This is Heading size 3</h3>
        <h4>This is Heading size 4</h4>
        <h5>This is Heading size 5</h5>
        <h6>This is Heading size 6</h6>
    </body>
</html>
```

This example HTML script provides an alternative way of producing the same output as that produced previously using ASP.NET. What is interesting here is that if you were to click the right mouse button on your ASP.NET web page and select the View Source option from the pop-up menu, you will find that the code used to produce the page was the same as that above, without any ASP.NET instructions in sight. What happened to the ASP.NET instructions? Well, when the page was requested from the server, the server processed the ASP.NET instructions, and created HTML script. This is then sent to the browser for display.

Error Messages

If things have not gone well and you have made a mistake you will be presented with an error message, similar to that shown in Figure 3.3.

If you didn't accidentally create an error then you can deliberately create this error message yourself by changing the ASP.NET line in your script from:

```
<% Dim intHeading As Integer %>
```

to:

```
<% Dim intBHeading As Integer %>
```

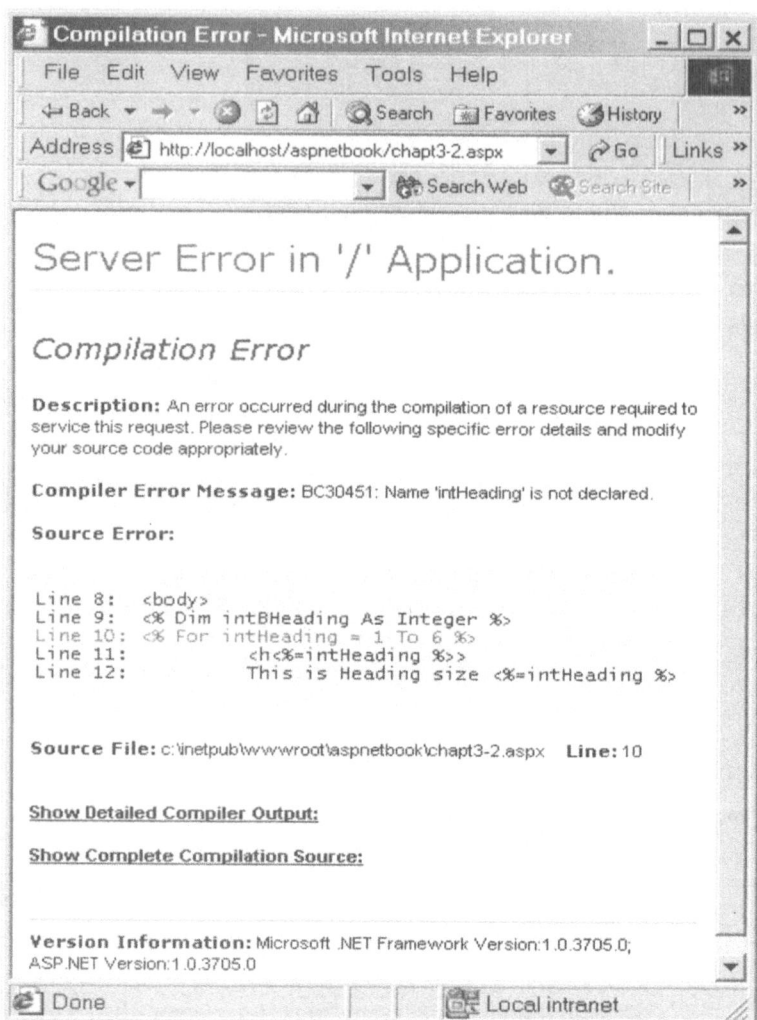

Figure 3.3 An error message.

Notice that the error reporting provides a clear indication that the variable **intHeading** has not been declared. This is correct, as we have deliberately renamed it to **intBHeading**.

Static and Dynamic Web pages

We have mentioned before that HTML documents are static as they can only display the same content each time they are accessed. Dynamic web pages on the other hand, are web pages that may change each time they are accessed. In general, a dynamic web page is one whose content is produced automatically by a program each time the page is accessed.

A standard for such programs emerged in the early days of the web. The standard, known as the Common Gateway Interface (programs which comply with it are often known as CGI scripts) basically specifies how a web server will pass data to a program when it executes. CGI scripts can be written in a wide variety of languages including PERL, C, and TCL etc.

But how do CGI scripts work? Well, consider the diagram in Figure 3.4.

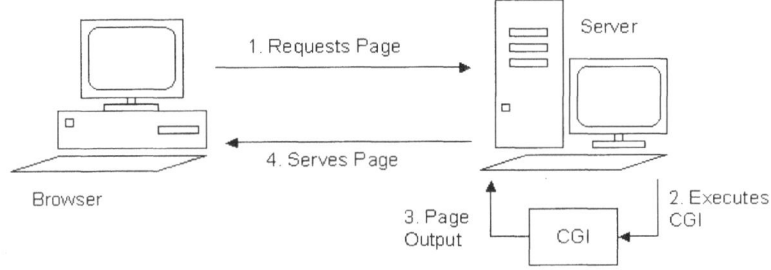

Figure 3.4 CGI scripts

In Figure 3.4 CGI processing begins when a browser requests a document (which in this case is a CGI application) from a web server. The browser doesn't care whether the requested page is a static HTML document or a CGI script, it just sends the request to the web server. The web server recognises the request for a CGI script and executes the specific CGI application. The CGI script does whatever it has been programmed to do and outputs some standard HTML. This output is served to the browser for displaying as a web page.

One problem with CGI applications is that the HTML instructions, which control the format of the dynamic information produced by the applications, tend to get lost amid the program code. This effect makes it more difficult to produce attractive, easy to use dynamic web pages and also has an impact on maintenance.

How is ASP.NET Different?

The ASP.NET approach to dynamic web pages is different in one major respect; instead of the HTML being embedded into program code, ASP.NET program code is embedded into the HTML document, see Figure 3.5.

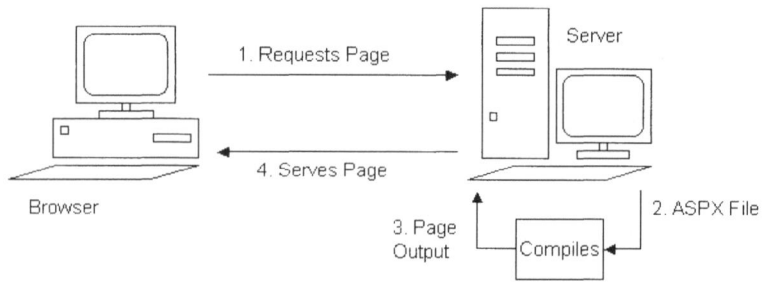

Figure 3.5 ASP.NET scripts

Figure 3.5 illustrates that when a browser requests an ASP.NET page, the web server will first compile the page if this is the first time that the ASP.NET page has been requested or if a programmer has made a change to the code. The compiled page is then executed. Any HTML in the script is passed straight back to the browser, but any program code therein is executed and any output fed back to the browser as well.

The important thing to note here is that it is the responsibility of the ASP.NET programmer to ensure that the ASP.NET code creates valid HTML syntax otherwise the browser will be unable to display it correctly. Consider the following script:

```
<%@Page Language="VB" Debug="True" %>

<html>
    <head>
    <title>chapt3-4.aspx Bad HTML Output</title>
    </head>

    <body>
    <% Dim intHeading As Integer %>
    <% For intHeading = 1 To 6 %>
        <h <%=intHeading %>>
        This is Heading size <%=intHeading %>
        </h<%=intHeading %>>
    <% Next %>
    </body>
</html>
```

This simple script is designed to produce the same output as that illustrated in Figure 3.2. Unfortunately, the programmer has made an error:

```
<h <%=intHeading %>>
```

Note that this line has an extra space in it, just after the <h. Because this mistake does not affect the VB.NET syntax in any way, this will not cause a compiler error.

However if you were to enter this program and save it in the IIS web server directory, the output produced would look like Figure 3.6.

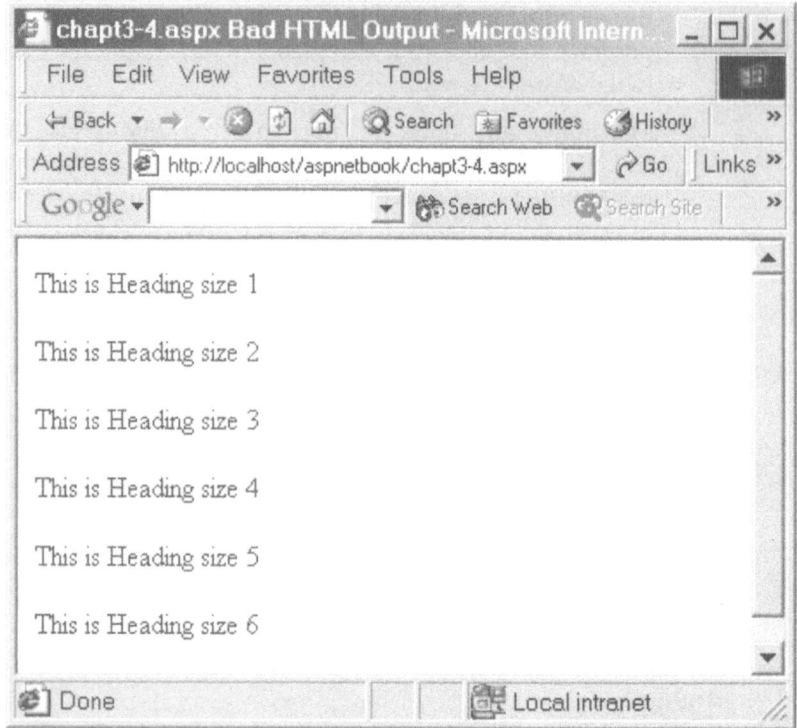

Figure 3.6 Output as a result of incorrect HTML syntax

So far, we have introduced ASP.NET and described how it works. We have also introduced some related technology. In the remainder of this chapter we shall examine the use of the VB.NET language a little more closely.

Formatting ASP.NET Instructions

The VB.NET language is quite tolerant of how you wish to lay out its instructions. For example, this:

```
<% Dim intHeading As Integer %>
<% intHeading = 45 %>
```

```
<%=Heading %>
```

> is a perfectly acceptable way of including these instructions within a HTML document. However, the following is also equally valid:

```
<%
Dim intHeading As Integer
intHeading = 45
%>
<% =intHeading %>
```

> Note that we cannot have a single set of delimiters around all three instructions, as the last instruction <% =intHeading %> is a special case and requires its own delimiters in order to correctly output the value it holds.

Jumping in and out of ASP.NET

> You can jump in and out of ASP.NET within a HTML document whenever you like. Consider the following example:

```
<%@Page Language="VB" Debug="True" %>

<html>
     <head>
     <title>chapt3-5.aspx Jumping in and out of ASP.NET</title>
     </head>

     <body>
     <% Dim strComment As String %>
     This is static HTML<br>
     <% StrComment = "This is generated with ASP.NET<br>" %>

     This is static HTML<br>
     <% =StrComment %>
     This is static HTML<br>
     <% =StrComment %>
     </body>
</html>
```

In this example, a number of instances of ASP.NET code have been inserted at different points within the HTML document. The output from this example is illustrated in Figure 3.7.

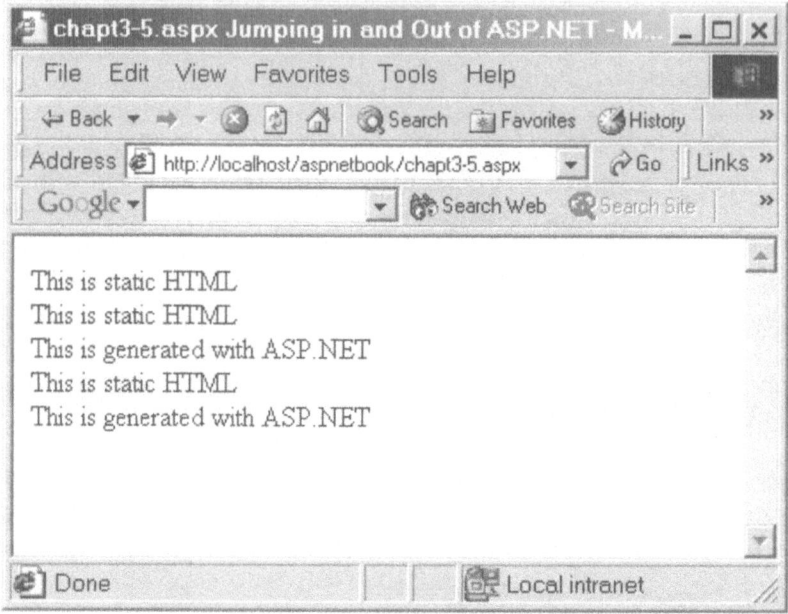

Figure 3.7 Output produced using ASP.NET and standard HTML

Most ASP.NET scripts will be embedded within HTML documents as it is easier to write them this way than to have the ASP.NET generate each and every line of HTML.

The Response.Write Object

In addition to the <%=VariableName%> method of outputting variable values ASP.NET has an inbuilt method called **Response.Write**. Response.Write allows you to output information to a web page. Here is an example:

```
Response.Write("Hello, this is some text")
```

This method would display the text **"Hello, this is some text"** on the web page. The method can also be used to output variable values and combinations of text and variables, as illustrated in the following example:

```
<%@Page Language="VB" Debug="True" %>

<html>
    <head>
    <title>chapt3-6.aspx Writing to a page</title>
    </head>
    <body>
    <%

    Dim intAge As Integer
    intAge = 34
    %>
    Can display text like this<br>
    <%
    Response.Write("Can also output text like this<br>")
    Response.Write("Can also display variables, such as intAge=" & intAge)
    %>
    </body>
</html>
```

Note that in the above example, the following line is used to display some text and a variable value:

```
Response.Write("Can also display variables, such as intAge=" & intAge)
```

The & character is used to concatenate the string and variable value together.

Summary

In this chapter we have introduced the basics of the ASP.NET environment. We have described how to create an ASP.NET script using Visual Basic (VB.NET) and insert this in a HTML document. We have also described how ASP.NET works.

By now you should be able to create a HTML document and embed a very simple ASP.NET script inside it. You should also be able to save this file with the file extension .aspx and view the output using a web browser. In the next chapter we shall provide an overview of the VB.NET language.

Chapter 4

VB.NET Basics

Introduction

This chapter provides a brief introduction to the VB.NET language. VB.NET is the language that we are using to create our ASP.NET applications. This chapter is meant to provide a basic introduction to the language. If you require a more detailed introduction we suggest that you read Essential VB.NET *fast*, which is part of this series of books.

Variables

Variables are defined in VB.NET using the **Dim** keyword followed by the name of the variable (which must be unique) and finally an indication of the variable type, for example:

```
<%
Dim intAge As Integer
%>
```

This defines a variable called **intAge** of type **Integer**. Variable names in VB.NET are not case sensitive.

Assigning values to variables

VB.NET supports assigning variables by value. Assigning by value means that when an expression (value or variable) is assigned to a variable, the value of the expression is copied into the destination variable. The syntax for assigning a variable by value is as follows:

```
<%
Dim intAge As Integer
intAge = 45
%>
```

In the above code fragment, the variable intAge is defined and then assigned the value 45.

Explicit Variable Declarations

While the previous examples of variables in VB.NET have a Dim statement somewhere in the code before the variables are used, this is not an actual requirement. If you start using a variable that you have not defined, VB.NET simply creates this for you. While this may at first seem like a wonderful feature, it is very bad programming practice indeed. In complex programs trying to find errors is made more difficult if variables aren't properly defined before their use. The good thing is that VB.NET can come to our rescue by allowing us to force variables to be defined before you use them. To activate this feature you simply include an additional option in the page header called Explicit and set this to true:

```
<%@Page Language="VB" Debug="True" Explicit="True" %>
```

From now on all the examples in this book will use this option.

Different Types of Variables

VB.NET provides excellent support for different types of variables, a total of 12 in all, which are listed in Table 4.1 along with the size in bytes that each variable type uses.

The reason VB.NET supports so many different types of variables is because there are many different types of data that each variable type is more suited to handle. For example, some variables store real numbers, some integers.

Table 4.1 VB.NET supported variable types

Type	Size in bytes
Byte	1
Short	2
Integer	4
Long	8
Single	4
Double	8
Decimal	16
Char	2
Boolean	2
Date	8
Object	Varies
String	Varies

Integer Numbers

VB.NET supports four different types of variables, which can store integer variables and these are listed in Table 4.2.

Table 4.2 Integer types and value ranges

Type	Min	Max
Byte	0	255
Short	-32,678	32,767
Integer	-2,147,483,648	2,147,483,647
Long	-9,223,372,036,854,775,808	9,223,372,036,854,775,807

The variable types in Table 4.2 are **Byte, Short, Integer** and **Long**. The difference between each of them is in the maximum and minimum size of number, which can be stored.

We would suggest that you should not only give variables meaningful names, which reflect the data they contain, but you should also include as part of the name a prefix, which indicates the type of variable it is.

Table 4.3 lists the four different integer data types, the suggested prefix and an example of a variable name using the prefix.

Table 4.3 Integer types and prefixes

Type	Suggested Prefix	Example
Byte	Byte	ByteAge
Short	Short	ShortYear
Integer	Int	IntPopulation
Long	Lng	LngStarsinGalaxy

Floating point (real) numbers

VB.NET provides support for real numbers, also known as floating point numbers in some programming languages, and these types are listed in Table 4.4.

Table 4.4 Floating point types and ranges of values

Type	Min	Max
Single	-3.402,823,5 E38	3.402,823,5 E38
Double	−1.797,693,134,862,32 E308	1.797,693,134,862,32 E308
Decimal	-79,228,162,414,264,337, 593,543,950,335	79,228,162,414,264,337, 593,543,950,335

Table 4.5, lists the suggested prefix for each of these types.

Table 4.5 Floating point suggested prefixes

Type	Suggested Prefix	Example
Single	Sng	SngSalary
Double	Dbl	DblPi
Decimal	Dec	DecBudget

Other data types

In addition to integer and floating point types VB.NET supports a collection of other variable types, which we have grouped together under the uninspiring title of other data types. These are listed in Table 4.6.

Table 4.6 Other data type prefixes

Type	Suggested Prefix	Example
Char	Char	charLetter
Boolean	Bool	boolGender
Date	Date	dateToday
Object	Obj	objPerson
String	Str	strName

Table 4.6 also provides a suggested prefix for each variable type and provides an example of their use.

Declaring and Initialising Together

You may have noticed that in the previous examples variables have been declared and then values assigned to them on separate lines. There is no need to do it this way, and another equally valid and some would argue tidier method exists:

```
<%
Dim charLetter As Char = "A"
Dim boolGender As Boolean = 1
%>
```

Constants

A constant is a variable which when given a value for the first time cannot be subsequently changed. To create a constant you use the Const keyword instead of Dim. Examples of constant declarations are:

```
Const sngTax As Single = 17.5
Const intMonths As Integer = 12
```

By using a variable name instead of a number you can make your code more readable.

Automatic Conversion

Variables can be converted from one type to another. Consider the following example:

```
Dim intAge As Integer
Dim sngAgeMonths As Single
intAge = 47
sngAgeMonths = intAge + 0.3
```

In this example, an Integer variable intAge is declared and assigned the value 47. Another variable sngAgeMonths is declared of type Single and this is assigned the value of intAge + 0.3.

Standard Conversions

Although, as we have just seen, automatic variable conversion is possible, this is bad practice and can result in some weird and unpredictable effects. A much better way of doing variable type conversion is to use the inbuilt functions, which were created for doing exactly this. To stop automatic conversion we can add another option to the page header called Strict. When Strict="True" is included automatic conversion is banned:

```
<%@Page Explicit="True" Language="VB" Strict="True" Debug="True" %>
```

All examples will use Strict="True" from now on.

Conversion Functions

Table 4.7 lists the different inbuilt functions, which have been provided for you to convert from one variable type to another.

Table 4.7 Variable type conversion functions

Convert to	Function
Byte	CByte()
Short	CShort()
Integer	CInt()
Long	CLng()
Single	CSng()
Double	CDbl()
Decimal	CDec()
String	CStr()
Char	CChar()
Boolean	CBool()
Date	CDate()

You will see these functions used a lot in the examples in later chapters.

Strings

Strings can be defined using the **String** variable type:

```
Dim strName As String = "Simon"
```

Strings are a collection of characters (letters, symbols and numbers) that together form the string. Strings require the use of double quotation mark characters "" to indicate the start and end of a string.

Expression, Operand & Operator

A simple expression is:

```
intAge = 5
```

Here, the variable **intAge** is assigned the constant value **5**. In this example, **5** is the expression.

An operand is simply something that is operated upon. In an expression like **34 - sngPi**, one operand is a constant (**34**), the other a variable (**sngPi**). Operators allow you to manipulate or "operate upon" variables and constants.

Arithmetic Operators

VB.NET supports seven different arithmetic operators, which are listed in Table 4.8.

Table 4.8 Arithmetic operators

Name	Symbol	Example	Description
Addition	+	$5 + 2 = 7$	Add 5 and 2
Subtraction	-	$5 - 2 = 3$	Subtract 2 from 5
Multiplication	*	$5 * 2 = 10$	Multiply 5 and 2
Division	/	$7 / 2 = 3.5$	Divide 7 by 2
Exponentiation	^	$4 \wedge 3 = 64$	Multiply 4 * 4 * 4
Modulus	Mod	$5 \text{ Mod } 3 = 2$	Remainder of dividing 5 by 3
Integer Division	\	$7 \setminus 2 = 3$	Divide 7 by 2 (giving integer)

Assignment Operators

Don't consider "=" to be an "equal to" character, it should be read as an "assign to" character. The simplest use of the assignment operator is:

```
intVar = 56;
```

This reads "the value **56** is assigned into the variable **intVar**". ASP.NET also supports a number of "combined operators", which are listed in Table 4.9.

Table 4.9 Combined operators

Operator	Example	Description
+=	intA += 3	intA = intA + 3
-=	intA -= 2	intA = intA - 2
*=	intA *= 3	intA = intA * 3
/=	intA /= 2	intA = intA / 2
^=	intA ^= 3	intA = intA ^ 3
\=	intA \= 2	intA = intA \ 2
&=	strA &= strB	strA = strA & strB

Comparison Operators

Comparison operators are used to compare expressions both logically and arithmetically. Table 4.10 illustrates the comparison operators supported.

Table 4.10 Comparison operators

Meaning	Operator	Example
Equal	=	intA = intB
Not equal	<>	intA <> intB
Less than	<	intA < intB
Greater than	>	intA > intB
Greater than or equal to	>=	intA >= intB
Less than or equal to	<=	intA <= intB

Comparison operators are used a great deal in VB.NET and some examples of their use can be found later in this chapter in the section on Loops.

Logical Operators

A number of logical operators are supported, which are listed in Table 4.11.

Table 4.11 Logical operators

Name	Example	Description
And	intA And intB	True if both intA and intB are true.
Or	intA Or intB	True if either intA or intB are true.

The logical operators are used to combine the results of comparison operators according to the laws of Boolean algebra. In VB.NET a value of 0 is used to represent a logical *false* condition and a value of 1 for a logical *true*.

Loops and Ifs

VB.NET supports a number of constructs, which allow us to control the execution of programme statements.

If Then

The If Then is a simple construct, which enables a conditional execution of script statements. The basic syntax is:

```
If condition Then
Statement(s)
End If
```

When an If Then expression is reached the computer evaluates the condition and if it is true then the statements between the Then and End If are executed. If it is false then the statements are not executed. For example:

```
If intSalary > 45000
```

```
        strText = "Big Earner!"
End If
```

The above script fragment checks if **intSalary** is greater than **45000** and if so assigns the text "**Big Earner!**" to variable **strText**.

Expanding If Then with Else

Sometimes you may wish to have one or many statements executed if an expression is true, and another set of statements if the expression is false. The **Else** statement is used in conjunction with the **If** statement to achieve this. The syntax for use of the **Else** statement is:

```
If condition Then
        Expressions
Else
        Expressions
End If
```

If conditions allow you to combine a number of conditional checks together using the Boolean **OR** and **AND** operators.

Elseif

A condition can also be applied to the **Else** part of an **If** statement by using an **Elseif** construct. For example:

```
If intDay = 1 Or intDay = 7 Then
        strText = "the fantastic Weekend"
Elseif intDay = 6
        strText = "Friday, hurray!"
Else
        strText = "a horrible Workday"
End If
```

Select Statement

The **Select** statement is similar to a collection of **If** statements. The **Select** statement is used when you wish to compare a variable against a number of different values and execute different code depending on its value. You can implement this using a number of **If** statements, but the code can become complex and difficult to understand. Let us consider an example:

```
Select Case intMonth
Case 1
    strText = "January"
Case 2
    strText = "February"
Case 3
    strText = "March"
Case 4
    strText = "April"
Case 5
    strText = "May"
End Select
```

The above example implements a **Select** statement which checks the case for the variable **intMonth** being equal to the values 1 to 5 and assigning the relevant month into the **strText** variable, which is then displayed.

Do While and Do Until Top Testing

Do While and **Do Until** are simple forms of loop. In the case of the **Do While** loop, statements inside the loop are executed until the loop expression is false. The syntax for the top testing form of this loop construct is:

```
Do While Condition
    Statements
Loop
```

```
Do Until Condition
      Statements
Loop
```

With the **Do Until** loop the statements in the loop are performed until the condition is met. Both top tested loops have the condition tested at the beginning of the loop construct. This means that the program may either enter the loop and process the statements within, or the condition may evaluate to false (or true) immediately and no statements inside the loop are executed. This type of loop is referred to as 0, 1 or Many loop as the statements inside the loop may be executed zero, one or many times.

Do While and Do Until Bottom Testing

The **Do While** and **Do Until** loops can be employed using a bottom checking condition. The syntax for **Do While** loop construct is:

```
Do
      Statements
Loop While Condition
```

The **Do Until** bottom tested loop has a similar syntax:

```
Do
      Statements
Loop Until Condition
```

The only difference between the bottom checking loops and the top checking ones is where the condition is checked for true or false. In a bottom checking loop the condition is checked at the bottom of the loop, after the statements within the loop have been executed once. Because of this, bottom checking loops are known as a one or many loops, as the statements within are executed at least once, and perhaps many times.

For loop and step

The For loop is another form of loop, the simplest syntax of which is:

```
For Variable = starting-from To ending-at
     Statements
Next
```

With a For loop a variable is used within the loop to keep track of the number of times the loop has been executed. A starting-from value is used to declare the starting value of this loop variable. The loop will iterate from this value until it reaches the value declared in ending-at.

The For loop has an additional keyword that can be used to control the value that the loop variable is incremented each time around the loop. This is known as the Step value:

```
For intCount = 1 To 6 Step 2
```

In this example the loop will iterate from 1 to 6 but will be incremented by 2 each time. Thus, the intCount values will be 1, 3 and 5:

Arrays

An array is an indexed sequence of one or more variables, which share a common name. VB.NET supports arrays and these are defined in much the same way as variables:

```
Dim strName(10) As String
```

In the above example a String array has been created which is 11 elements in size. Each element can hold a unique value. In defining an array, elements start from 0 to the number specified in the parentheses, making a total of 11 in this example. Array elements are easily referenced:

```
strName(3) = "Simon Stobart"
```

```
strName(5) = "Norman Parrington"
strName(6) = "Liz Hall"
```

Subroutines

Subroutines are blocks of code which have a unique name. When the subroutine is called, the code inside the subroutine is performed. When complete the computer returns back to the place from which the subroutine was called.

In ASP.NET subroutines must be placed inside a special element, the HTML <script> element:

```
<script runat="server">
      ' subroutines here
</script>
```

Note that the <script> tag has a special **runat="server"** attribute to indicate that the script inside the element is ASP.NET script. It is important where you insert the <script> elements as they cannot go anywhere. In fact the <script> elements must be placed before the <body> tag in your page. As only ASP.NET code can be inserted inside the <script> element you should not try and use the <% %> delimiters. In fact the compiler will not let you anyway.

The keyword to define the start and end of a subroutine is:

```
Sub Name (any-arguments)
..
End Sub
```

The name of the subroutine must be unique. You cannot have two subroutines in the same page with the same name. Any arguments, which are to be passed to the subroutine, are specified in parentheses after the subroutine name. To call a subroutine the syntax is:

```
SubName
```

Let's examine an example:

```
<%@Page Explicit="True" Language="VB" Strict="True" Debug="True" %>
<html>
     <head>
     <title>chapt4-1.aspx Simple Subroutine</title>
     </head>

     <script runat="server">
          Sub DisplayHeading
                  Response.Write("<h1>This is a Heading</h1>")
          End Sub
     </script>
     <body>
     <%
     DisplayHeading
     DisplayHeading
     %>
     </body>
</html>
```

Let's examine this script. The subroutine has been placed inside the <script> element before the <body> element:

```
<script runat="server">
     Sub DisplayHeading
     Response.Write("<h1>This is a Heading</h1>")
     End Sub
</script>
```

Note, because we wish to output something to the web page and we are inside a subroutine then we must use the **Response.Write** method, mentioned in Chapter 3. We have to do this because we cannot use the <%= %> element inside the <script> element. Two calls to the subroutine are included in the body of the page:

```
<%
DisplayHeading
DisplayHeading
%>
```

This results in two headings being written to the web page. Not very interesting, so let's try and make things a little better.

Subroutines and Arguments

Subroutines can accept arguments. Consider the following modification of our previous example:

```
<%@Page Explicit="True" Language="VB" Strict="True" Debug="True" %>
<html>
    <head>
    <title>chapt4-2.aspx Subroutines with Arguments</title>
    </head>

    <script runat="server">
        Sub DisplayHeading (intSize As Integer, strtext As String)
            Response.Write("<h" & intSize & ">" & strText & "</h" & intSize & ">")
        End Sub
    </script>
    <body>
    <%
    DisplayHeading (2, "This is a heading")
    DisplayHeading (1, "Which can be adjusted for size")
    DisplayHeading (3, "and for the text shown!")
    %>
    </body>
</html>
```

The subroutine above is the same as the previous example except that it has two arguments:

```
Sub DisplayHeading (intSize As Integer, strtext As String)
    Response.Write("<h" & intSize & ">" & strText & "</h" & intSize & ">")
End Sub
```

The first argument variable intSize is used to set the size of the displayed heading. The second argument contains the text, which is output. This time the subroutine is invoked three times, passing different arguments to demonstrate the power of the subroutine:

```
DisplayHeading (2, "This is a heading")
DisplayHeading (1, "Which can be adjusted for size")
DisplayHeading (3, "and for the text shown!")
```

Functions

Functions are almost the same as subroutines except that they also return values. Like subroutines functions are placed inside a <script> element and have the same restrictions. The keyword to define the start and end of a function is:

Function Name (any-arguments) As Type

..

End Function

In addition to the keyword **Function**, function declarations need to define the return type of the value the function will return. To return a value the keyword **Return** is used inside the function definition:

Return (value)

The following is an example of a function that receives a argument and returns a value:

```
<%@Page Explicit="True" Language="VB" Strict="True" Debug="True" %>
<html>
    <head>
    <title>chapt4-3.aspx Functions</title>
    </head>

    <script runat="server">
        Function LeapYear (intYear As Integer) As Integer
        Dim intLeap As Integer

        If ((((intYear Mod 4) = 0) And ((intYear Mod 100) <> 0)) Or ((intYear Mod
400) = 0)) Then
                intLeap = 1
        Else
                intLeap = 0
        End If
        Return (intLeap)
        End Function
    </script>
    <body>
```

```
<%
Dim intYear As Integer
Dim intAns As Integer
Dim strText As String

For intYear = 1990 To 2002
      intAns = LeapYear(intYear)
      If intAns = 1 Then
            strText = " is a Leap Year"
      Else
            strText = " is not a Leap Year"
      End If
      %>
      <%=intYear & strText%><br>
      <%
Next
%>
</body>
</html>
```

In fact this script implements a function called **LeapYear**:

```
<script runat="server">
      Function LeapYear (intYear As Integer) As Integer
      Dim intLeap As Integer

      If (((((intYear Mod 4) = 0) And ((intYear Mod 100) <> 0)) Or ((intYear Mod 400) = 0))
Then
            intLeap = 1
      Else
            intLeap = 0
      End If
      Return (intLeap)
      End Function
</script>
```

This function receives an **Integer** value that represents a calendar year. Through the use of a complex **If** statement it determines if the year is a leap year or not. If it is a leap year the Integer value 1 is return otherwise a value of 0 is returned.

Exiting a Function or Subroutine

If you ever need to exit a function or subroutine you can use the command:

```
Exit Sub
```

to jump out of a subroutine or

```
Exit Function
```

to leave a function. The following script fragment provides an example of doing this:

```
Function WeekDay(intDay As Integer) As Integer
    If intDay > 7 Or intDay < 1 Then
        Exit Function
    End If
```

In this example a function receives an integer representing a day of the week. The function checks if the value is between 1 and 7 and if not the function exits immediately.

Summary

This chapter has provided an overview of VB.NET syntax, variable types and constructs, which will be used in the following chapters. There is a lot more to the VB.NET language than what we have described here. For example, we have not had space to examine how to construct your own VB.NET objects and classes. However, the ASP.NET framework comes with a large number of already created objects and in the next chapter we shall examine some of these.

Chapter

5

ASP.NET
Objects

Introduction

ASP.NET comes with a large number of predefined objects and classes that we can use to good effect in our applications. We shall introduce some of these in this chapter and provide some examples of their use.

Response Object

We have previously encountered the **Response** object and used one of its methods: **Response.Write** to output text to a HTML page from within a subroutine or function. The **Response** object has other methods which are available, one of which is the **Response.Redirect** method, the syntax of which is:

```
Response.redirect("Webpage")
```

The **Response.redirect()** method allows you to redirect a user to another web page. Consider the following example:

```
<%@Page Explicit="True" Language="VB" Strict="True" Debug="True" %>
<html>
    <head>
    <title>chapt5-1.aspx Redirecting</title>
    </head>

    <body>

    <%
    Dim intNum As Integer
    Dim strSite As String

    Randomize
    intNum = CInt((Rnd * 3) + 1)

    Select case intNum
    Case Is = 1
```

```
            strSite = "chapt4-1.aspx"
    Case Is = 2
            strSite = "chapt5-1.aspx"
    Case Is = 3
            strSite = "chapt6-1.aspx"
    End Select

    Response.Redirect(strSite)
    %>
    </body>
</html>
```

The above script defines two variables called **intNum** and **strSite**. It then uses a facility of the language which we have not introduced thus far, the Random number facility. The first part of the random number generator is **Randomize**.

Randomize

This command instructs the computer to "seed" the random number generator. Why do we need this? Well, when the computer generates random numbers it uses a complex formula, which always starts at the same place. This means that the random numbers will always occur in a set sequence, which is not that useful. The **Randomize** statement forces the computer to begin at a random location and thus results in what appears to be random numbers. The next line creates a random number:

```
intNum = CInt((Rnd * 3) + 1)
```

This statement uses the (**Rnd * 3**) command to generate a random number between 0 and 2. Adding 1 to this means the numbers generated are between 1 and 3. The **CInt** function is used to convert the returned number into an integer. The next section of code implements a **Select** statement, which sets the value of **strSite** to a different web page depending on the value of **intNum**:

```
Select case intNum
```

```
Case Is = 1
     strSite = "chapt4-1.aspx"
Case Is = 2
     strSite = "chapt5-1.aspx"
Case Is = 3
     strSite = "chapt6-1.aspx"
End Select
```

Finally, the following object method invocation causes the web page stored in **strSite** to be loaded in the browser:

```
Response.Redirect(strSite)
```

Request Object

The **Request** object has been designed to allow data to be passed from one web page to another. You may have seen when you have visited various pages on the web that the web page address (known as the URL) is displayed in the location window of the browser:

```
www.mywebpage.com
```

But in some cases you will see a URL something like this:

```
www.mypage.com?strName=Simon
```

This URL not only has the name of the web page but also has a question mark followed by some additional data, in this case:

```
strName=Simon
```

This is a mechanism by which information can be passed from one page to another and in this example a variable called **strName** has been assigned a value of "Simon". Multiple variables can be passed in this fashion by using the ampersand character to separate them, for example:

```
www.mypage.com?strName=Simon&intAge=65&sngHeight=5.11
```

The following is an example of a script, which creates and assigns three variables and passes them to a second web page:

```
<%@Page Explicit="True" Language="VB" Strict="True" Debug="True" %>
<html>
    <head>
    <title>chapt5-2.aspx Passing Variables</title>
    </head>

    <body>

    <%
    Dim intAge As Integer = 35
    Dim strName As String = "Simon Stobart"
    Dim sngHeight As Single    = 5.11

    Response.write("The values of the variables are<br>Name: " & strName & ", Age: "
& intAge & " and Height: " & sngHeight)

    Response.write("<br><br><a href='chapt9-3.aspx?strName=" & strName &
"&intAge=" & intAge & "&sngHeight=" & sngHeight & "'>Click here to send data.</a>")

    %>
    </body>
</html>
```

Don't click on the hyperlink just yet as we haven't written the web page which is going to receive these variables. Examining the above script we see that it defines three variables called **strName**, **intAge** and **sngHeight,** and assigns these some values. These are then displayed. A hyperlink is created which includes these data values. The next stage is to create a script, which is able to receive and use these variables.

The object that is used to access variables which are passed between web pages is called **Request** and the particular method is the **QueryString** method. The syntax is as follows:

```
Request.QueryString("VariableName")
```

The following is an example of a script which illustrates its use:

```
<%@Page Explicit="True" Language="VB" Strict="True" Debug="True" %>
<html>
      <head>
      <title>chapt5-3.aspx Response QueryString</title>
      </head>

      <body>

      <%
      Dim intAge As Integer
      Dim strName As String
      Dim sngHeight As Single

      intAge = CInt(Request.QueryString("intAge"))
      strName = CStr(Request.QueryString("strName"))
      sngHeight = CSng(Request.QueryString("sngHeight"))

      Response.write("The values of the variables are<br>Name: " & strName & ", Age: "
& intAge & " and Height: " & sngHeight)

      %>
      </body>
</html>
```

The above script defines three variables but does not assign them any values. The **Request.QueryString** method is used to access each of the variables and store them in the variables defined within this script:

```
intAge = CInt(Request.QueryString("intAge"))
strName = CStr(Request.QueryString("strName"))
sngHeight = CSng(Request.QueryString("sngHeight"))
```

The values of the variables are then displayed.

Further Request Object Methods

Finally, it is worth noting that the **Request** object has a number of additional methods that can be accessed to provide useful information about the client accessing the web page. These are listed in Table 5.1

Table 5.1 Further request object methods

Method	Description
Url	URL of web page
UrlReferrer	URL of previous page.
UserHostName	Users Host Computer Name
UserHostAddress	Users Host IP Address

The following script illustrates their use:

```
<%@Page Explicit="True" Language="VB" Strict="True" Debug="True" %>
<html>
      <head>
      <title>chapt5-4.aspx Extra Request Methods</title>
      </head>

      <body>

      <%
      Dim objCarDrivers As HashTable = New Hashtable
      Dim uriUrl As Uri
      Dim uriUrlReferrer As Uri
      Dim strUserHostName As String
      Dim strUserHostAddress As String

      uriUrl = Request.Url
      uriUrlReferrer = Request.UrlReferrer
      strUserHostName = Request.UserHostName
      strUserHostAddress = Request.UserHostAddress

      Response.Write("Url: ")
      Response.Write(uriUrl)
      Response.Write("<br>Referrer: ")
```

```
        Response.Write(uriUrlReferrer)
        Response.Write("<br>HostName: " & strUserHostName)
        Response.Write("<br>HostAddress: " & strUserHostAddress)

        %>
        </body>
</html>
```

Note in the above example that the methods .Url and .UrlReferrer return types Uri.

Request Object Browser Object

Hidden inside the **Request** object is another object called **Browser.** This object provides really useful information about the browser that is being used to access the web page. Table 5.2 lists the different methods which can be examined to provide useful information.

Table 5-2 Browser object methods

Method	Description
Browser	The information passed from the browser to the Server
Cookies	Supports Cookies
Frames	Supports Frames
JavaApplets	Supports Java Applets
JavaScript	Supports JavaScript
Platform	The operating system being used
Tables	Supports Tables
Type	The name and version number of the browser
Version	Version number of the browser

The following script provides an example of these methods in use:

```
<%@Page Explicit="True" Language="VB" Strict="True" Debug="True" %>
<html>
    <head>
    <title>chapt5-5.aspx Request Browser Object</title>
    </head>
```

```
<body>

<%
Dim objCarDrivers As HashTable = New Hashtable
Dim strBrowser As String
Dim strPlatform As String
Dim strType As String
Dim strVersion As String

Dim boolAns As Boolean

StrBrowser = Request.Browser.Browser
StrPlatform = Request.Browser.Platform
StrType = Request.Browser.Type
Strversion = Request.Browser.Version

Response.Write("Browser: " & strBrowser)
Response.Write("<br>Platform: " & strPlatform)
Response.Write("<br>Type: " & strType)
Response.Write("<br>Version: " & strVersion)

If Request.Browser.Cookies = True Then
      Response.Write("<br>Supports Cookies")
Else
      Response.Write("<br>Does not support Cookies")
End If

If Request.Browser.Frames = True Then
      Response.Write("<br>Supports Frames")
Else
      Response.Write("<br>Does not support Frames")
End If

If Request.Browser.JavaApplets = True Then
      Response.Write("<br>Supports Java Applets")
Else
      Response.Write("<br>Does not support Java Applets")
End If

If Request.Browser.JavaScript = True Then
      Response.Write("<br>Supports JavaScript")
Else
```

```
            Response.Write("<br>Does not support JavaScript")
      End If

      If Request.Browser.Tables = True Then
            Response.Write("<br>Supports Tables")
      Else
            Response.Write("<br>Does not support Tables")
      End If

      %>
      </body>
</html>
```

ArrayList Class

The ArrayList class is a class that works in a similar way to an array, but provides some much needed methods to make array handling much easier and useful. To begin using the ArrayList we need to create an instance of the class using the syntax:

```
Dim objMotorCars As ArrayList = New ArrayList
```

This creates an object called **objMotorCars** of type ArrayList. The ArrayList class has a number of methods defined which we can use with our object. The first of these is the **Add** method which allows us to add items to the ArrayList. The syntax is:

```
objMotorCars.Add("Item to Add")
```

The item to add to the ArrayList is provided as a **String**. The next method we shall introduce is the **Count** method, which returns an **Integer** indicating the number of items stored in the ArrayList object:

```
intNumCars = objMotorCars.Count
```

You can access individual items stored in the ArrayList just like an array, by using a subscript, for example:

```
strMyCar = CStr(objMotorCars(2))
```

The above will return the third item stored. Remember that like arrays the first element is numbered zero. However, ArrayList allows us to search its contents with more ease than with an array. For example, the .Contains method will return a Boolean value of true or false to indicate if an item is presently stored in the ArrayList:

```
boolCarThere = objMotorCars.Contains("Ford Focus")
```

The above will check to see if the objMotorCars object contains a car called "Ford Focus". We can find the position in the ArrayList of an item using the .IndexOf method:

```
intCarPos = objMotorCars.IndexOf("Ford Focus")
```

We can delete an item from the ArrayList by either using the .RemoveAt method, which uses the subscripted position of the item:

```
objMotorCars.RemoveAt(2)
```

or, by using the .Remove method to access a named item:

```
objMotorCars.Remove("Ford Focus")
```

We can remove all items from the ArrayList by using the .Clear method. We can sort the items into order using the .Sort method and we can reverse the items in the list using the .Reverse method:

```
objMotorCars.Clear
objMotorCars.Sort
objMotorCars.Reverse
```

Let's see an example of using the ArrayList class:

```
<%@Page Explicit="True" Language="VB" Strict="True" Debug="True" %>
<html>
    <head>
    <title>chapt5-6.aspx Using ArrayList</title>
    </head>
    <body>
    <h1>Using the ArrayList Class</h1>
    <%
    Dim strMyCar As String
    Dim intCarCount As Integer
```

```
Dim intCarPos As Integer
Dim boolCarThere As Boolean
Dim objMotorCars As ArrayList = New ArrayList
objMotorCars.Add("Ford Focus")
objMotorCars.Add("Ford Ka")
objMotorCars.Add("Toyota Avensis")
objMotorCars.Add("Mazda 323")
objMotorCars.Add("Renault Clio")
objMotorCars.Add("Nissan Micra")
objMotorCars.Add("Vauxhall Vectra")
objMotorCars.Add("BMW 318")
intCarCount = objMotorCars.Count
Response.Write("There are " & intCarCount & " Cars in the list.<br>")
boolCarThere = objMotorCars.Contains("Ford Focus")
If boolcarThere = True Then
        intCarPos = objMotorCars.IndexOf("Ford Focus")
        Response.Write("The Ford Focus is in the list at postion " & intCarPos &
".<br>")
        objMotorCars.Remove("Ford Focus")
        Response.Write("I have now deleted the Ford Focus from the list.<br>")
        intCarCount = objMotorCars.Count
        Response.Write("There are " & intCarCount & " Cars in the list.<br>")
End If
objMotorCars.Sort
Response.Write("I have now sorted the list.<br>")
strMyCar = CStr(objMotorCars(0))
Response.Write("The first car in the list is:" & strMyCar & ".<br>")
%>
</body>
</html>
```

The output from this script is shown in Figure 5.1.

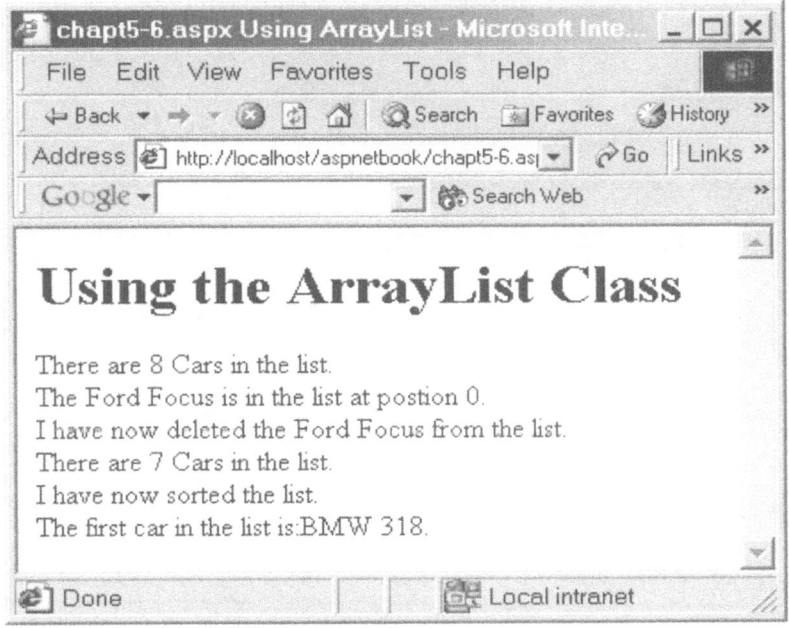

Figure 5.1 *Using the ArrayList*

HashTable Object

Another useful object is called the **HashTable**. The **HashTable** works in a similar way to the **ArrayList** but it not only allows you to store items in the table but also to give them a name. When you want to access the information you can do so by referring to the items by name. A **HashTable** is created in the same way as an **ArrayList**:

```
Dim objCarDrivers As HashTable = New Hashtable
```

Items can be added to the **HashTable** object using the **.Add** method, specifying the name of the item and its value:

```
objCarDrivers.Add("Name", "Value")
```

To access an item in the **HashTable** you simply provide its
name and the value is returned:

```
objCarDrivers("Name")
```

Consider the following example:

```
<%@Page Explicit="True" Language="VB" Strict="True" Debug="True" %>
<html>
    <head>
    <title>chapt5-7.aspx Using the HashTable</title>
    </head>

    <body>

    <%
    Dim objCarDrivers As HashTable = New HashTable
    Dim strDriver As String

    objCarDrivers.Add("Ford Focus", "Liz Hall")
    objCarDrivers.Add("Ford Ka", "Billy Lee")
    objCarDrivers.Add("Toyota Avensis", "Ian Walker")
    objCarDrivers.Add("Mazda 323", "Simon Stobart")
    objCarDrivers.Add("Renault Clio", "Hayley West")
    objCarDrivers.Add("Nissan Micra", "Kevin Hinds")
    objCarDrivers.Add("Vauxhall Vectra", "Alan Fell")
    objCarDrivers.Add("BMW 318", "Gemma West")

    strDriver = CStr(objCarDrivers("Ford Ka"))

    Response.Write(strDriver & " drives a Ford Ka")
    %>
    </body>
</html>
```

The output from the above script is shown in Figure 5.2.

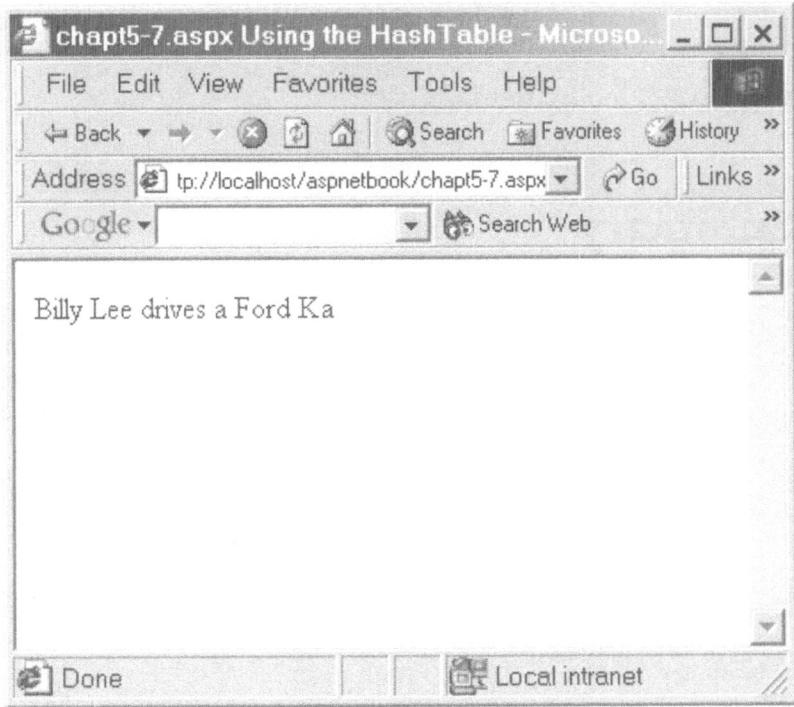

Figure 5.2 Using the *HashTable*

In the above example a **HashTable** called **objCarDrivers** is created and populated with some data describing the cars and their drivers. The **HashTable** is then queried to determine who drives a **"Ford Ka"** and the result stored in a string variable **strDriver**. This is then displayed:

```
strDriver = CStr(objCarDrivers("Ford Ka"))
```

Like **ArrayList** the **HashTable** object has a number of other methods which can be used. These include:

```
ObjCarDrivers.Remove("Name")
```

that allows an individual entry to be removed. Also:

```
intNum = ObjCarDrivers.Count
```

returns the number of items stored. To see if any of the item names is set to a certain value:

```
boolAns = ObjCarDrivers.ContainsKey("Name")
```

Summary

This chapter has introduced a number of inbuilt objects and classes with have been provided as part of the ASP.NET environment to make your programming life easier. By the end of this chapter you should be able to access and make use of these objects. In the next chapter we shall examine how we can interact with the user using ASP.NET forms.

Chapter 6

Interacting with the User

Introduction

Forms are used in HTML documents to accept data from a web page user. The original purpose of the HTML form mechanism was to transmit the data back to the server to be processed by a CGI application. This chapter examines how you can use forms and access form data in ASP.NET.

ASP.NET and Forms

If you have had experience of creating and using forms before and even of writing CGI scripts, you may be thinking that you have got a big head-start with this chapter. But be warned, ASP.NET forms and HTML forms are quite different in the way they work. Our advice would be to forget all you know about HTML form processing and approach this chapter as though you had never come across forms before.

Server Controls

When creating ASP.NET the developers looked at traditional application programs which run under Microsoft Windows, and considered the controls which allow these programs to interact with users. Such controls include textboxes, buttons and checkboxes. It seemed obvious to the ASP.NET developers that since these controls work well for Windows applications, there was no reason why they should employ the same technology for ASP.NET. Furthermore, as ASP.NET runs on the server then the control used on the web page should also run on the server. This concept has led to the development of

ASP.NET web forms. These are simply web pages which use ASP.NET server controls.

Simple Form Processing

To begin let's create a web page that uses some ASP.NET server controls. One example is shown below:

```
<%@Page Explicit="True" Language="VB" Strict="True" Debug="True" %>
<html>
     <head>
     <title>chapt6-1.aspx Simple Form</title>
     </head>

     <body>
     <h1>Welcome to your first ASP Form</h1>

     <form runat="server">
     <asp:textbox id="Name" runat="server"/><br>
     <asp:button text="Ok" runat="server"/>
     </form>

     </body>
</html>
```

The above script creates a very simple form, consisting of a single **Textbox** field and a **Button**. The **Form** element looks similar to that of a standard HTML form, except that it has the attribute **runat="server"** which indicates that it is a ASP.NET web form which is to be processed at the server:

```
<form runat="server">
```

Inside the form element are two ASP.NET server controls. The first one:

```
<asp:textbox id="Name" runat="server"/>
```

specifies a **Textbox**, with an **id** of **"Name"**. This will allow us to refer to the data contained in the textbox later. Once again the **runat="server"** attribute indicates that the element will be processed at the server. Notice that the element ends with />. This is a relatively new HTML construct with allows us to put the open and close tags of an element together. We could if we wished write the tags as:

```
<asp:textbox id="Name" runat="server"></asp:textbox>
```

but this is a little more long winded. The second ASP.NET server control is:

```
<asp:button text="Ok" runat="server"/>
```

This defines a **Button** with the **text="Ok"** attribute indicating what text will appear on the button when it is displayed.

Don't enter any data into the form just yet or click the **Ok** button as we have not created the part of the script to handle the event of someone interacting with the form.

ASP.NET Server Control Events

In order to get things a little more interesting we need to implement some server control event handling code. An event is something that occurs with an application, usually when a user interacts with it, by clicking a button for example. The following script enhances the previous one in order to show what we mean:

```
<%@Page Explicit="True" Language="VB" Strict="True" Debug="True" %>
<html>
	<head>
	<title>chapt6-2.aspx Simple Form Event Handling</title>
	</head>

	<script runat="server">

		Sub ButtonClick(Sender As Object, E As EventArgs)
			If Len(Name.Text) = 0
				Message.Text = "I don't know who you are!"
```

```
            Else
                    Message.Text = "Hello, " & Name.Text
            End If

        End Sub

    </script>

    <body>
    <h1>Welcome to your first ASP Form</h1>

    <form runat="server">
    Please enter your name:
    <asp:textbox id="Name" runat="server"/>
    <asp:label id="Message" runat="server"/><br>
    <asp:button text="Ok" onclick="ButtonClick" runat="server"/>

    </form>

    </body>
</html>
```

Figure 6.1 illustrates the output from this script.

The above script has a number of changes to the previous one so let's examine each of these. The first change we need to examine is with the <asp:button control:

```
<asp:button text="Ok" onclick="ButtonClick" runat="server"/>
```

This control has a new attribute onclick="ButtonClick". This attribute captures the event of the user clicking on the button and when this occurs control is returned to the server, which then runs the subroutine "ButtonClick".

The "ButtonClick" subroutine has been coded as follows:

```
<script runat="server">
    Sub ButtonClick(Sender As Object, E As EventArgs)
        If Len(Name.Text) = 0
            Message.Text = "I don't know who you are!"
        Else
            Message.Text = "Hello, " & Name.Text
        End If
```

```
        End Sub
</script>
```

Figure 6.1 An ASP.NET web form

The subroutine has two arguments, **Sender** and E. All subroutines written to respond to events such as a button click require these. While we need to include them we don't have to use them, so for now we shall ignore them. Inside the "**ButtonClick**" subroutine is a simple **If** condition, which checks the value of **Name.Text**. **Name.Text** is the value that was entered in the **Textbox** called **Name** on the form contained. The number of characters in this string (all data from forms is passed as strings) is calculated using the **Len** function. The **Message.Text** object is then set to one of two different strings depending on the size of **Name.Text**:

```
If Len(Name.Text) = 0
        Message.Text = "I don't know who you are!"
Else
        Message.Text = "Hello, " & Name.Text
End If
```

The final change is the addition of a new ASP.NET control on the form:

```
<asp:label id="Message" runat="server"/><br>
```

A **label** control is designed to display information on a form. In this case it has the **id="Message"**. This has been created to display the value **Message.Text** set in our subroutine.

The Page Object

The **Page** object represents the entire web page and consists of a number of useful methods and properties to assist you in handling web forms. The **Page** object contains an event called **Page_Load**. **Page_Load** is automatically run each time the page is loaded. Consider the following example:

```
<%@Page Explicit="True" Language="VB" Strict="True" Debug="True" %>
<html>
      <head>
      <title>chapt6-3.aspx Page_Load Event</title>
      </head>

      <script runat="server">

            Sub Page_Load(Sender As Object, E As EventArgs)

            SurName.Text = SurName.Text
            FirstName.Text = FirstName.Text
```

```
        End Sub

    </script>

    <body>
    <h1>Welcome to my ASP Form</h1>

    <form runat="server">
    Firstname:<br>
    <asp:textbox id="SurName" runat="server"/><br>
    Surname:<br>
    <asp:textbox id="FirstName" runat="server"/><br>

    <asp:button text="Ok" onclick="ButtonClick" runat="server"/>

    </form>

    </body>
</html>
```

In the above example a **Page_Load** subroutine has been included which sets the values of **SurName** and **FirstName** back to the values they were when the form was completed:

```
Sub Page_Load(Sender As Object, E As EventArgs)
    SurName.Text = SurName.Text
    FirstName.Text = FirstName.Text
End Sub
```

This allows us to retain the data that was entered on the form even after the form has been submitted. What would also be useful is if we could display something in the form fields when the page was first displayed, not afterwards. This can be accomplished using the **IsPostBack** variable.

IsPostBack

IsPostBack is a ASP.NET variable that is false when a page is first loaded by a browser and then is set to true for all times the page is loaded. For an example of its use consider the following script fragment:

```
Sub Page_Load(Sender As Object, E As EventArgs)
If IsPostBack = False Then
        SurName.Text = "Required"
                FirstName.Text = "Required"
        Else
                SurName.Text = SurName.Text
                FirstName.Text = FirstName.Text
        End If
End Sub
```

In this example, the **Page_Load** subroutine has been rewritten to include an **IsPostBack** variable. An **If** statement checks if this is the first time the page has been loaded by a browser. If false the values of **SurName** and **FirstName** are set to required. If **IsPostBack** is true then the form variables are set to themselves.

The following example illustrates how **Page_Load** can be used to maintain a page access count:

```
<%@Page Explicit="True" Language="VB" Strict="True" Debug="True" %>
<html>
        <head>
        <title>chapt6-5.aspx Simple Counter</title>
        </head>

        <script runat="server">

                Sub ButtonAdd(Sender As Object, E As EventArgs)
                Dim intCount As Integer
                intCount = CInt(Count.Text)
                intCount += 1
                Count.Text = CStr(intCount)
                End Sub

                Sub ButtonMinus(Sender As Object, E As EventArgs)
                Dim intCount As Integer
                intCount = CInt(Count.Text)
                intCount -= 1
                Count.Text = CStr(intCount)
                End Sub
```

```
            Sub Page_Load(Sender As Object, E As EventArgs)

            If IsPostBack = False Then
                    Count.Text = "0"
            End If
            End Sub

    </script>

    <body>
    <h1>Welcome to my ASP Counter Form</h1>

    <form runat="server">
    <asp:label id="Count" runat="server"/><br>

    <asp:button text="+" onclick="ButtonAdd" runat="server"/>

    <asp:button text="-" onclick="ButtonMinus" runat="server"/>

    </form>

    </body>
</html>
```

The above script contains a simple form, which consists of a **Label** to display the counter and two buttons:

```
<form runat="server">
<asp:label id="Count" runat="server"/><br>

<asp:button text="+" onclick="ButtonAdd" runat="server"/>
<asp:button text="-" onclick="ButtonMinus" runat="server"/>

</form>
```

The buttons have the characters "+" and "-" on them and by clicking the +'ve button will add 1 to the counter, while clicking the –'ve button will decrease the counter by one. A **Page_Load** subroutine checks if this is the first time the page has been loaded and if so sets the value of **Count.Text** to zero:

```
Sub Page_Load(Sender As Object, E As EventArgs)
```

```
If IsPostBack = False Then
    Count.Text = "0"
End If
End Sub
```

Two button subroutines have been included to handle the events of clicking on the two buttons:

```
Sub ButtonAdd(Sender As Object, E As EventArgs)
Dim intCount As Integer
intCount = CInt(Count.Text)
intCount += 1
Count.Text = CStr(intCount)
End Sub

Sub ButtonMinus(Sender As Object, E As EventArgs)
Dim intCount As Integer
intCount = CInt(Count.Text)
intCount -= 1
Count.Text = CStr(intCount)
End Sub
```

Both subroutines basically do the same thing. They declare an Integer variable called intCount and convert the Count.Text value to an Integer and store this in intCount. intCount is then incremented (or decremented depending on the subroutine) and the value converted back to a string and stored in Count.Text for display on the form.

Figure 6.2 illustrates the output from the above script.

Passing non form variables between pages

In the previous example we illustrated how a form variable could be passed from one page load to another. But what about a standard ASP.NET variable? Can we pass variables from one web page to another?

Figure 6.2 Simple counter

Consider the following example:

```
<%@Page Explicit="True" Language="VB" Strict="True" Debug="True" %>
<html>
    <head>
    <title>chapt6-6.aspx Retaining Non-form variables</title>
    </head>

    <script runat="server">

        Dim intGlobalCount As Integer
```

```
                    Sub ButtonAdd(Sender As Object, E As EventArgs)
                    Dim intCount As Integer
                    intCount = CInt(Count.Text)
                    intCount += 1
                    Count.Text = CStr(intCount)
                    intGlobalCount += 1

                    End Sub

                    Sub Page_Load(Sender As Object, E As EventArgs)

                    If IsPostBack = False Then
                         Count.Text = "0"
                         intGlobalCount = 0
                    End If

                    End Sub

          </script>

          <body>
          <h1>Welcome to your first ASP Form</h1>

          <form runat="server">
          <asp:label id="Count" runat="server"/><br>

          <asp:button text="Ok" onclick="ButtonAdd" runat="server"/>

          </form>
          The value of intGlobalCount is <%=intGlobalCount%>

          </body>
</html>
```

The above example retains the **Count** variable counter from the previous example, although it can now only be increased for the sake of simplicity. A global variable is defined:

```
Dim intGlobalCount As Integer
```

The value of which is displayed on the web page:

```
The value of intGlobalCount is <%=intGlobalCount%>
```

When the page is first loaded both the global variable and the form variable are set to zero:

```
If IsPostBack = False Then
        Count.Text = "0"
        intGlobalCount = 0
End If
```

Each time the form button is clicked the **intGlobalCount** button is incremented by 1, which is shown in Figure 6.3.

Unfortunately, this example doesn't work. Why? Well, unfortunately global variables do not retain their value between page loads. However. there is a way to solve this problem using **ViewState** which we will explore next.

ViewState

In ASP.NET a web page contains a hidden object called **ViewState**. **ViewState** is used to store all information about the web page, for example: what controls there are, what values these controls are set to, etc. In addition to this the **ViewState** can be used to store any variables which we wish to remember between page loads. To store a variable in the **ViewState** we use the syntax:

```
ViewState("name") = variablename
```

Figure 6.3 Output from retaining non-form data

To access the variable from the **ViewState** we use the syntax:

```
Variablename = ViewState("name")
```

The previous has been modified to take advantage of the **ViewState** facility:

```
<%@Page Explicit="True" Language="VB" Strict="True" Debug="True" %>
<html>
    <head>
    <title>chapt6-7.aspx using ViewState</title>
    </head>
```

```
<script runat="server">

    Dim intGlobalCount As Integer

    Sub ButtonAdd(Sender As Object, E As EventArgs)
    Dim intCount As Integer
    intCount = CInt(Count.Text)
    intCount += 1
    Count.Text = CStr(intCount)
    intGlobalCount += 1
    ViewState("intGlobalCount") = intGlobalCount

    End Sub

    Sub Page_Load(Sender As Object, E As EventArgs)

    If IsPostBack = False Then
        Count.Text = "0"
        intGlobalCount = 0
    Else
        intGlobalCount = Cint(ViewState("intGlobalCount"))
    End If

    End Sub

</script>

<body>
<h1>Welcome to your first ASP Form</h1>

<form runat="server">
<asp:label id="Count" runat="server"/><br>

<asp:button text="Ok" onclick="ButtonAdd" runat="server"/>

</form>
The value of intGlobalCount is <%=intGlobalCount%>

</body>
</html>
```

The above script uses the **ViewState** property to store the value of the variable **intGlobalCount**, each time a page is loaded.

Page_PreRender

Before we finish this chapter we should introduce another event handler, the **Page_PreRender**. This event occurs just before the page is sent back to the browser and this can be used to store any variables in the **ViewState**, for example:

```
Sub Page_PreRender(Sender As Object, E As EventArgs)
ViewState("intGlobalCount") = intGlobalCount
End Sub
```

Summary

This chapter has introduced ASP.NET forms. Forms are an essential part of any on-line ASP.NET development and we have only just begun to examine what form features are supported with ASP.NET. In the following chapter we shall introduced some more form controls.

Chapter 7

Examining Web Server Controls

Introduction

In this chapter we shall continue to further examine the various user interface controls that were introduced in the previous chapter. We shall see that there are a number of further properties that each of these controls supports to allow us more control over what they do and how they appear.

The Textbox

The Textbox is one of the most commonly used user interface controls. However, there is a lot more to the textbox than was previously described. In fact there are a large number of different properties that we can use to affect the appearance of the Textbox. These properties are listed in Table 7.1.

We shall examine each of these different properties in turn providing some examples of their use.

Forecolor and Backcolor

Forecolor specifies the foreground colour of the control text and Backcolor specifies the backgound colour. The following is an example of the use of these properties:

```
<%@Page Explicit="True" Language="VB" Strict="True" Debug="True" %>
<html>
    <head>
    <title>chapt7-1.aspx Forecolor and Backcolor</title>
    </head>

    <body>
    <form runat="server">
```

```
<asp:textbox id="Address" forecolor="white" backcolor="blue" runat="server"/>

</form>
</body>
</html>
```

The above script produces an ASP.NET form. This form contains a single control, which specifies a **Textbox** with the foreground colour of white and the background colour of blue.

Table 7.1 Textbox control properties

Property	Description
Text	Text that is displayed
AutoPostBack	The page should return to the server when the textbox has been modified
BackColor	The background colour of the control
BorderColor	The border colour of the control
BorderStyle	The style of the border surrounding the control
Columns	Width of the textbox in columns
Rows	Height of the textbox in rows
Enabled	The control is enabled
ForeColor	The colour of the text string
Height	Height of the control
Width	Width of the control
Font-Name	Font typeface
Font-Size	Size of the text displayed
Font-Bold	Font is bold
Font-Underline	Font is underlined
Font-Italic	Font is italic
MaxLength	The number of characters which can be entered in the textbox
ReadOnly	The user cannot modify the text displayed in the textbox
TextMode	The type of textbox, single-line, password, multi-line
ToolTip	A pop-up window to provide some information about the control when the mouse pointer is held over it
Visible	The control is visible

But how do we know what different colours can be used with the **backcolor** and **forecolor** properties? Well, there are a large number of predefined colours and these are listed in Table 7.2.

Table 7.2 Different predefined colours

Colour	SubColour
Cyan	Light, Dark
Salmon	Light, Dark
Red	Dark, Indian, Orange, PaleViolet
Black	
Blue	Light, Dark, Medium, Alice, Cornflower, Dodger, Midnight, Powder, Royal
Green	Light, Dark, DarkOlive, Forest, Lawn, Lime, Pale, Yellow
SeaGreen	Light, Dark, Medium
White	Floral, Ghost, Navajo
Silver	
SkyBlue	Deep, Light
SpringGreen	Medium
Gray	Light, Dark, Dim
SlateBlue	Light
SlateGray	Dark, Light
SteelBlue	Light
Yellow	Light
Pink	Light, Deep, Hot
Brown	Rosey, Saddle, Sandy
Purple	Medium
Violet	Blue, Dark
Beige	
Tan	

Table 7.2 lists all of the predefined colour combinations. You can specify a colour such as:

```
Cyan
```

Or you can specify a specific sub-colour such as:

```
LightCyan
DarkCyan
```

Bordercolor and Borderstyle

Bordercolor allows you to alter the colour of the border surrounding a control. The colours, which can be used with

Bordercolor are the same as those with Forecolor and Backcolor and are listed in Table 7.2.

Borderstyle allows you to change the style of the border surrounding the control. Table 7.3 lists the different style effects that are available.

Table 7.3 Borderstyle effects

Style	Description
Solid	Solid line
None	No border
Inset	Inset border, sunken control
Outset	Outset border, sunken control
Groove	Grooved, sunken border
Ridge	Ridged, raised border

The following script provides an example of using these different controls:

```
<%@Page Explicit="True" Language="VB" Strict="True" Debug="True" %>
<html>
     <head>
     <title>chapt7-2.aspx Borderstyle</title>
     </head>

     <body>
     <form runat="server">
     Solid <asp:textbox id="Name1" borderstyle="Solid" runat="server"/><br>
     None <asp:textbox id="Name2" borderstyle="None" runat="server"/><br>
     Inset <asp:textbox id="Name3" borderstyle="Inset" runat="server"/><br>
     Outset <asp:textbox id="Name4" borderstyle="Outset" runat="server"/><br>
     Groove <asp:textbox id="Name5" borderstyle="Groove" runat="server"/><br>
     Ridge <asp:textbox id="Name6" borderstyle="Ridge" runat="server"/>
     </form>
     </body>
</html>
```

Figure 7.1 illustrates the output from the above script. Note that there is no button for you to submit the form, as this is only an example illustrating the different Textbox borders.

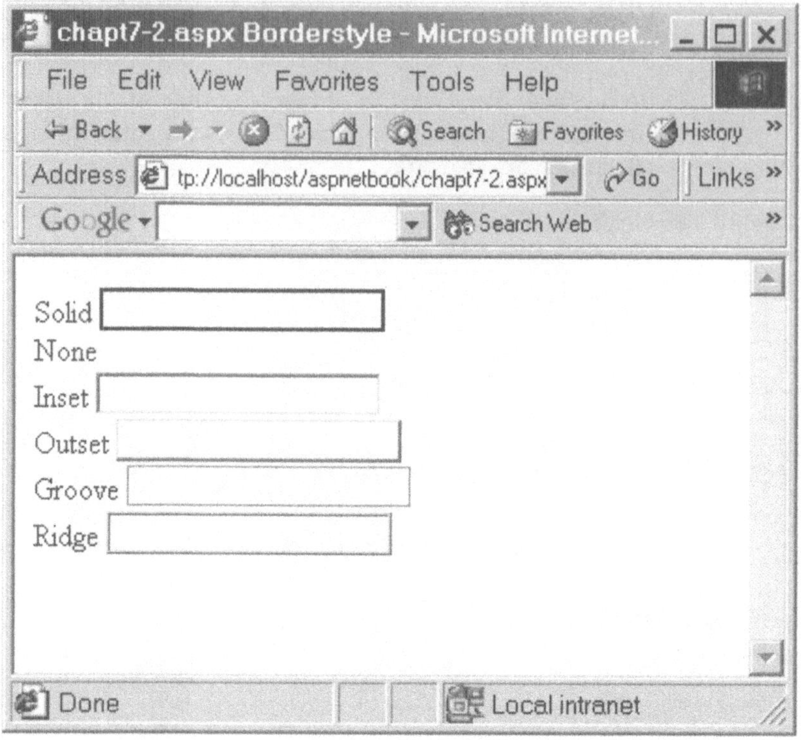

Figure 7.1 Different borders

Font Adjustment

There are a number of properties that allow you to specify the style of the font in the control. **Font-size**, **Font-name**, **Font-italic**, **Font-bold** and **Font-underline** can all be used to alter the style of the font.

With **Font-size** you specify the size of the text in points:

```
font-size="12pt"
```

In the case of **Font-name** the name of the font that you wish to use is specified:

```
font-name="Arial"
```

Finally, with **Font-italic**, **Font-bold** and **Font-underline** these are specified using a Boolean value of true or false:

```
font-italic="true"
font-bold= "false"
font-underline="true"
```

The following script illustrates an example of using these properties:

```
<%@Page Explicit="True" Language="VB" Strict="True" Debug="True" %>
<html>
    <head>
    <title>chapt7-3.aspx Fonts</title>
    </head>

    <body>
    <form runat="server">
    <asp:textbox id="Name1" text="Rockwell Font" font-Name="Rockwell"
runat="server"/><br>
    <asp:textbox id="Name2" text="Standard size 20pt" font-size="20pt"
runat="server"/><br>
    <asp:textbox id="Name3" text="Arial font" font-name="Arial" font-size="12pt"
runat="server"/><br>
    <asp:textbox id="Name4" text="Underlined" font-underline="true"
runat="server"/><br>
    <asp:textbox id="Name5" text="Italic" font-italic="true" runat="server"/><br>
    <asp:textbox id="Name6" text="Bold size 8pt" font-size="8pt" font-bold="true"
runat="server"/>
    </form>
    </body>
</html>
```

The output from this script is illustrated in Figure 7.2. Note that this example will only work if you have the different fonts that we have chosen. If you don't have the Rockwell font for example you can always edit the example and replace this font with a different font that you have installed on your system. Also notice that some of the controls do not look particularly attractive. The point here is just because you can do something, doesn't mean that you should.

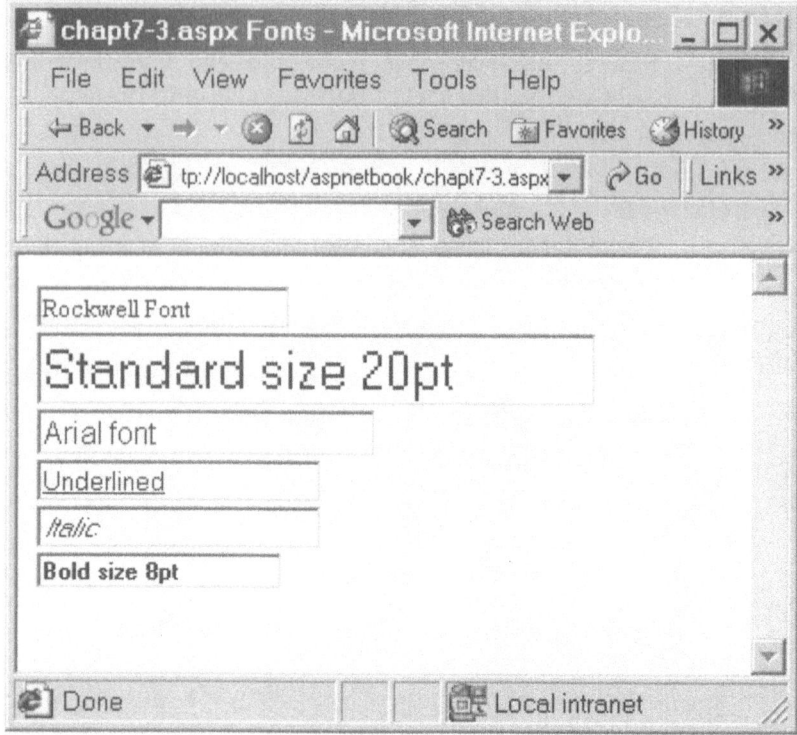

Figure 7.2 Fonts and sizes

Height and Width

Height and Width allow the height and width of your control to be specified in pixels. An example of their use can be seen in the following script:

```
<%@Page Explicit="True" Language="VB" Strict="True" Debug="True" %>
<html>
    <head>
        <title>chapt7-4.aspx Height and Width</title>
    </head>
```

```
      <body>
      <form runat="server">
      <asp:textbox id="Name1" text="Normal" runat="server"/><br>

      <asp:textbox id="Name2" text="Height=15" height="15" runat="server"/><br>

      <asp:textbox id="Name3" text="Width=100" width="100" runat="server"/><br>

      <asp:textbox id="Name4" text="Height=50, Width=200" height="50"
width="200" runat="server"/>
      </form>
      </body>
</html>
```

The above script creates a form with four different textboxes of different heights and widths.

Textmode

The **Textmode** property allows you to specify the three different modes of the **Textbox** control. These three modes are specified in Table 7.4.

Table 7.4 Textmode types

Type	Description
Singleline	Produce a textbox that allows only a single line of text to be entered
Multiline	Produce a textbox that allows multiple lines of text to be entered
Password	A single line textbox where the text entered is displayed as a series of asterisks, hiding what is typed from those viewing the screen

The following script illustrates the use of these properties:

```
<%@Page Explicit="True" Language="VB" Strict="True" Debug="True" %>
<html>
      <head>
      <title>chapt7-5.aspx textmode</title>
      </head>

      <body>
      <form runat="server">
```

```
    <asp:textbox id="Name1" textmode="singleline" text="Singleline"
runat="server"/><br>
    <asp:textbox id="Name2" textmode="password" text="Password"
runat="server"/><br>
    <asp:textbox id="Name3" textmode="multiline" text="Multiline"
runat="server"/>
    </form>
    </body>
</html>
```

The above script produces three textboxes. The first, a Singleline Textbox which is the default. The second, a Singleline password Textbox and finally, the third is a Multiline Textbox.

Columns, Rows and Maxlength

The Columns and Rows properties allow the size of the interface control to be specified in terms of the number of characters wide and as deep you wish it to appear. The Maxlength property allows you to limit the number of characters a user can enter into the Textbox. The following script illustrates the use of these properties:

```
<%@Page Explicit="True" Language="VB" Strict="True" Debug="True" %>
<html>
    <head>
    <title>chapt7-6.aspx columns, rows and maxlength</title>
    </head>

    <body>
    <form runat="server">
    <asp:textbox id="Name1" textmode="singleline" columns="20" text="20
columns" runat="server"/><br>
    <asp:textbox id="Name2" textmode="multiline" columns="30" rows="5"
text="30 columns, 5 rows" runat="server"/><br>
    <asp:textbox id="Name3" textmode="singleline" columns="40" maxlength="10"
text="40 columns, maxlength=10" runat="server"/>
    </form>
    </body>
</html>
```

The above script produces three textboxes. The first **Textbox** is set to a **Width** of 20 characters. The second is a **Multiline Textbox** of 30 characters wide and 5 lines deep. The third **Textbox** is 40 characters wide but has a maximum length of 10 characters. If you delete the text "**40 columns, maxlength=10**" and then try retyping the text, you will find that you are limited to entering a maximum of 10 characters.

Enabled / Visible

The **Enabled** and **Visible** properties take Boolean values of either true or false. The **Visible** property allows you to specify if a control is visible on the page. Controls are visible by default. When invisible the user cannot see the control, nor can they interact with it.

The **Enabled** control allows you to specify if a control can be interacted with or not. Controls are enabled by default. However, if a control is set to **Enabled="false"** then while the user can see it they are unable to interact with it. The following script provides an example of using these properties:

```
<%@Page Explicit="True" Language="VB" Strict="True" Debug="True" %>
<html>
     <head>
     <title>chapt7-7.aspx Enabled and Visible</title>
     </head>

     <body>
     <form runat="server">
     <asp:textbox id="Name1" textmode="singleline" text="Not enabled"
enabled="false" runat="server"/><br>
     <asp:textbox id="Name2" textmode="singleline" visible="false" runat="server"/>

     <asp:textbox id="Name3" textmode="singleline" text="Normal" runat="server"/>

     </form>
     </body>
```

```
</html>
```

The above script generates three textboxes, one visible, but not enabled, one not visible and one that is both visible and enabled. Note that the text in the **Enabled="false"** Textbox is displayed in grey, indicating that the text cannot be edited. Figure 7.3 illustrates the output from this script.

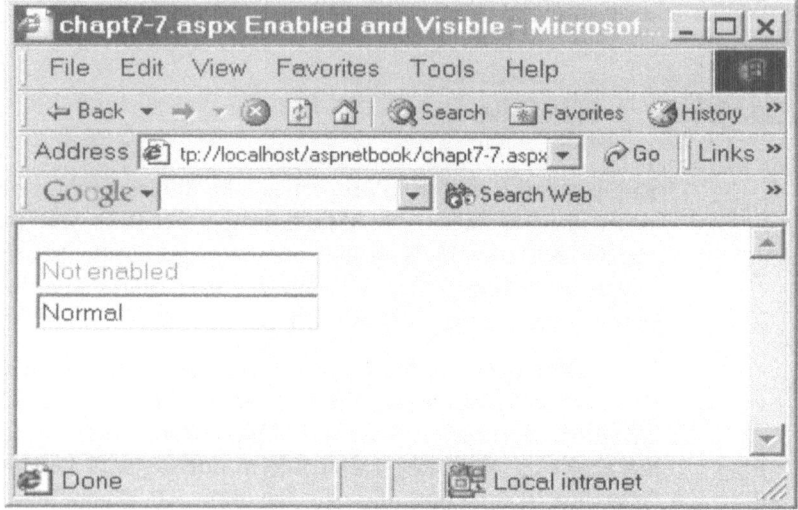

Figure 7.3 *Visible and enabled textboxes*

ReadOnly

The **ReadOnly** property allows you to specify if a user can edit a textbox or not. It takes a Boolean value of true or false. By default all textboxes are editable. This property is similar to the enabled property, but does not turn the text grey and thus it may be unclear to the user why they cannot edit the text. You should think carefully if you are going to use this property.

ToolTip

A ToolTip is a popup yellow box that appears when the user holds the mouse pointer over a control for a short period of time. It is designed to allow you to provide some useful information about the control to the user. The following script provides an example of its use:

```
<%@Page Explicit="True" Language="VB" Strict="True" Debug="True" %>
<html>
    <head>
    <title>chapt7-8.aspx ToolTip</title>
    </head>

    <body>
    <form runat="server">
    Surname: <asp:textbox id="Surname" textmode="singleline" tooltip="Your
Family Name" runat="server"/><br>
    Firstname: <asp:textbox id="Firstname" textmode="singleline" tooltip="Your
Firstname" runat="server"/><br>
    Address: <asp:textbox id="Address" rows="5" textmode="multiline"
tooltip="Your Address" runat="server"/>
    </form>
    </body>
</html>
```

The output from the above script is illustrated in Figure 7.4. If you hold the mouse pointer over one of the form controls then you will see the ToolTip appear.

AutoPostBack

The AutoPostBack property allows you to specify that in the event of a change to the property then the form data is submitted to the server for processing. The AutoPostBack property accepts the boolean values of true or false. Textbox controls are not set to AutoPostBack by default. In order to use this property effectively we need to also use an event called **TextChanged** that is invoked when the **Textbox** text has been altered.

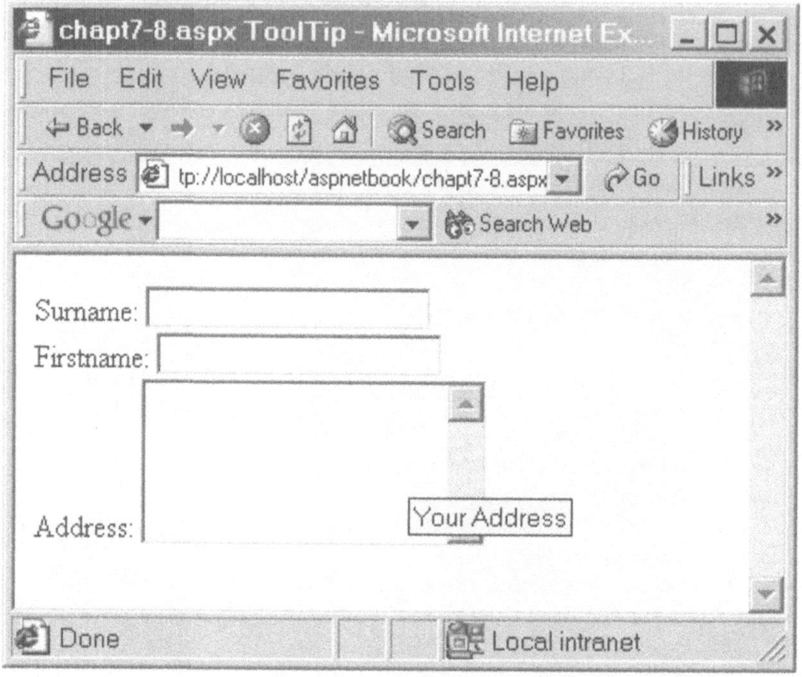

Figure 7.4 ToolTips

The format of this property and event is as follows:

```
<asp:textbox id="Id" autopostback="true" ontextchanged="callFunction"
runat="server"/>
```

The following script illustrates an example of using this property and event:

```
<%@Page Explicit="True" Language="VB" Strict="True" Debug="True" %>
<html>
    <head>
    <title>chapt7-9.aspx AutoPostBack</title>
    </head>

    <script runat="server">
```

```
Sub changecreditcard(Sender As Object, E As EventArgs)
    If CreditCard.Text = "No"
        CardNumber.Enabled = CBool("False")
        CardNumber.Text = "Not Required"
    Else
        CardNumber.Enabled = CBool("True")
        CardNumber.Text = ""
    End If
End Sub
</script>

<body>
<form runat="server">
Surname: <asp:textbox id="Surname" runat="server"/><br>

Firstname: <asp:textbox id="Firstname" runat="server"/><br>
Pay by credit card?: <asp:textbox id="CreditCard" autopostback="true"
ontextchanged="changecreditcard" runat="server"/><br>
Card Number: <asp:textbox id="CardNumber" runat="server"/><br>
</form>
</body>
</html>
```

In the above script a form is created which contains a number of server controls. One of these is a **Textbox** where the user types if they wish to pay by credit card or not. The form is not that sophisticated and assumes that the user will enter either Yes or No. The **Textbox** has an **AutoPostBack** property and when the user changes the contents of this control and moves to another control, then the form is returned to the server and the function **changecreditcard** will be invoked:

```
<asp:textbox id="CreditCard" autopostback="true"
ontextchanged="changecreditcard" runat="server"/>
```

The **changecreditcard** function checks to see if the value of **CreditCard** is equal to "No", then the value of the **CardNumber.Enabled** control is set to false and the text set to "Not Required":

```
Sub changecreditcard(Sender As Object, E As EventArgs)
    If CreditCard.Text = "No"
```

```
            CardNumber.Enabled = CBool("False")
            CardNumber.Text = "Not Required"
        Else
            CardNumber.Enabled = CBool("True")
            CardNumber.Text = ""
    End If
End Sub
```

If the **CreditCard.Text** is not equal to **"No"** then the control is re-enabled and the text **"Not Required"** is removed. Notice that this script illustrates the method by which we can change the values of control properties:

```
CardNumber.Enabled = CBool("False")
CardNumber.Text = "Not Required"
```

The output from this example is shown in Figure 7.5.

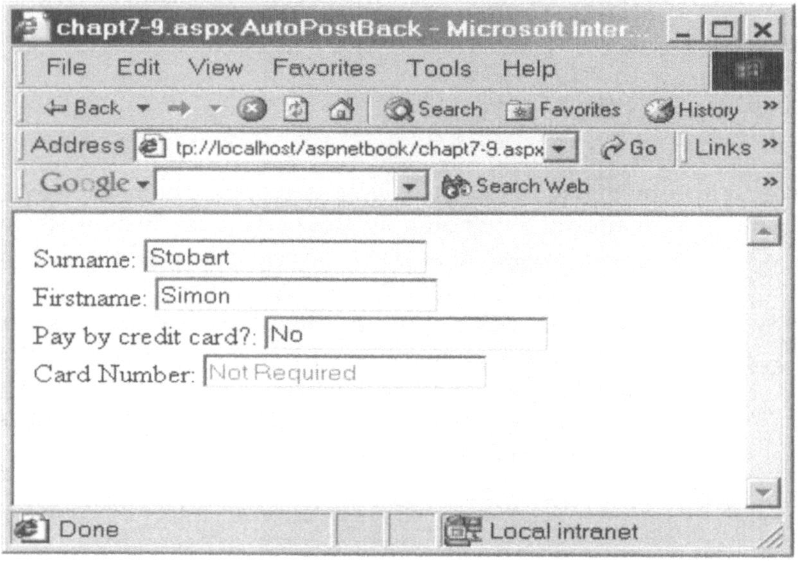

Figure 7.5 AutoPostBack output

The Label

We introduced the **Label** control in the previous chapter. While the **Label** control at first may appear limited in that it only allows text to be displayed on a ASP.NET form, like the **Textbox** control it has a number of properties which you can manipulate to make things a little more interesting. Table 7.5 lists the label control properties.

Table 7.5 Label control properties

Property	Description
Text	Text that is displayed
BackColor	The background colour of the control
BorderColor	The border colour of the control
BorderStyle	The style of the border surrounding the control
Enabled	The control is enabled
ForeColor	The colour of the text string
Height	Height of the control
Width	Width of the control
Font-Name	Font typeface
Font-Size	Size of the text displayed
Font-Bold	Font is bold
Font-Underline	Font is underlined
Font-Italic	Font in italic
ToolTip	A pop-up window to provide some information about the control which the mouse pointer is held over it
Visible	The control is visible

All of the **Label** properties in Table 7.5 have been covered previously with the **Textbox** control. These properties operate in exactly the same way as previously described.

The Button

The **Button** control was also introduced in the previous chapter. Like the **Textbox** and **Label** the **Button** control has a number of properties, which can affect its use. Table 7.6 lists these properties.

Table 7.6 Button control properties

Property	Description
Text	Text that is displayed
BackColor	The background colour of the control
BorderColor	The border colour of the control
BorderStyle	The style of the border surrounding the control
Enabled	The control is enabled
ForeColor	The colour of the text string
Height	Height of the control
Width	Width of the control
Font-Name	Font typeface
Font-Size	Size of the text displayed
Font-Bold	Font is bold
Font-Underline	Font is underlined
Font-Italic	Font in italic
ToolTip	A pop-up window to provide some information about the control which the mouse pointer is held over it
Visible	The control is visible

These properties all work in the same way as those previously shown using the **Textbox** control.

Summary

This chapter has re-examined the three basic user interface controls, the **Textbox**, the **Label** and the **Button**. Each of the properties that these different controls support has been described and examples of their use included. In the following chapter we shall introduce some further user interface controls.

Further Interface Controls

Introduction

This chapter examines some further interface controls that we have yet to consider. While in most cases we can get by with using textboxes, labels and buttons there are other controls that provide the developer with more scope to create richer, more interesting user interfaces. We shall examine each of these controls in turn, providing examples of their use.

CheckboxList

Checkboxes are a control, which allows you to present a series of options to the user allowing the selection of all options that apply. The syntax for the control is as follows:

```
<asp:checkboxlist id="name" runat="server">
    <asp:listitem>ItemDescription</asp:listitem>
    :

    :
</asp:checkboxlist>
```

The **checkboxlist** control surrounds a number of **listitem** controls. There is one **listitem** control for each item you wish to appear on the list. Consider the following example of a **checkboxlist**:

```
<%@Page Explicit="True" Language="VB" Strict="True" Debug="True" %>
<html>
    <head>
    <title>chapt8-1.aspx Checkboxes</title>
    </head>
    <script runat="server">
        Sub checkAnswer(Sender As Object, E As EventArgs)
            Dim intAnswers As Integer
            If fruits.Items(0).Selected = True
                intAnswers+=1
            End If
```

```
                    If fruits.Items(1).Selected = True
                        intAnswers-=1
                    End If
                    If fruits.Items(2).Selected = True
                        intAnswers+=1
                    End If
                    If fruits.Items(3).Selected = True
                        intAnswers+=1
                    End If
                    If fruits.Items(4).Selected = True
                        intAnswers-=1
                    End If
                    If intAnswers = 3
                        answer.text = "Correct"
                    Else
                        answer.text = "Wrong!"
                    End If
            End Sub
        </script>
        <body>
        <form runat="server">
        Which of these are fruits?<br>
        <asp:checkboxlist id="fruits" runat="server">
            <asp:listitem>Orange</asp:listitem>
            <asp:listitem>Potato</asp:listitem>
            <asp:listitem>Plum</asp:listitem>
            <asp:listitem>Apple</asp:listitem>
            <asp:listitem>Cabbage</asp:listitem>
        </asp:checkboxlist>
        <br><asp:label id="answer" runat="server"/>
        <br><asp:button id="select" text="Check Answer" onclick="checkAnswer"
runat="server"/>
        </form>
        </body>
</html>
```

The output from this script is shown in Figure 8.1. The form consists of three controls. The first is a **checkboxlist** which contains five **listitems**. The second is a **label** and the third is a **button**. When the button is clicked, control is returned to the server and the subroutine **checkAnswer** is invoked.

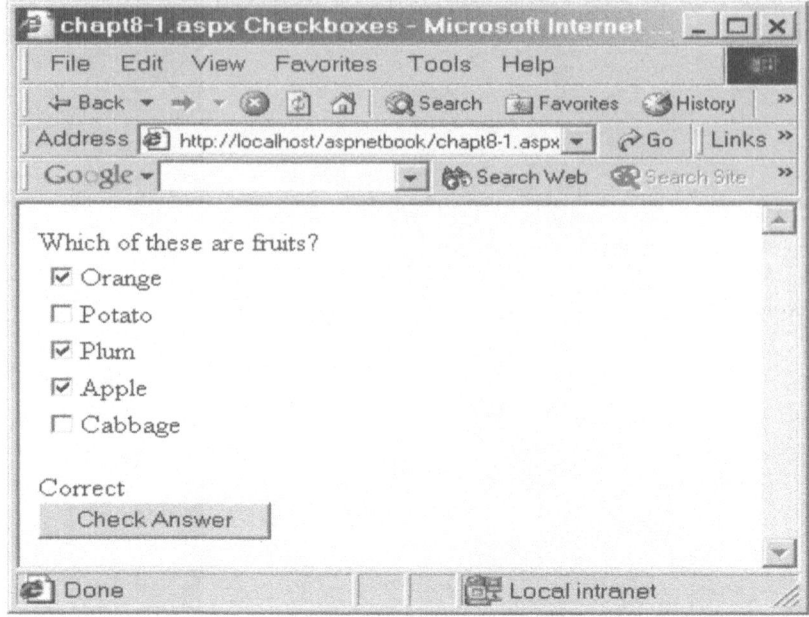

Figure 8.1 Checkboxes

Subroutine **checkanswer** consists of a series of **If** conditions which check each of the list Items to see if they have been selected. A running count of the correctly selected items is maintained and stored in **intAnswers**:

```
If fruits.Items(0).Selected = True
     intAnswers+=1
End If
If fruits.Items(1).Selected = True
     intAnswers-=1
End If
If fruits.Items(2).Selected = True
     intAnswers+=1
End If
If fruits.Items(3).Selected = True
     intAnswers+=1
End If
If fruits.Items(4).Selected = True
     intAnswers-=1
```

End If

The **CheckBoxList** control has a number of other properties that can be used. These are listed in Table 8.1.

Table 8.1 CheckBoxList control properties

Property	Description
Items(x).Selected	A boolean value indicating if the checkbox item has been selected.
AutoPostBack	The page should return to the server when the checkboxlist has been modified
Items(x).Text	The text which is used to label the checkboxlist item
Items(x).Value	The value associated with this item
Items.Add(String)	Add a new item to the end of the list
Items.Insert(x, String)	Insert a new item at position x
Items.Remove(String)	Remove item from the list
Items.Clear	Removes all items from the list
Items.Count	Count the number of items in the list
Items.RemoveAt(x)	Remove the list item at position X
CellPadding	The space around the checkbox and the table cell
CellSpacing	The space between each table cell
TextAlign	Whether the text appears to the left or right of the checkboxes
RepeatColumns	Number of columns used to display the checkboxes
RepeatDirection	The direction on the page that the checkboxes are displayed
RepeatLayout	Uses a HTML table to neatly display the checkboxes
BackColor	The background colour of the control
BorderColor	The border colour of the control
BorderStyle	The style of the border surrounding the control
Enabled	The control is enabled
ForeColor	The colour of the text string
Height	Height of the control
Width	Width of the control
Font-Name	Font typeface
Font-Size	Size of the text displayed
Font-Bold	Font is bold
Font-Underline	Font is underlined
Font-Italic	Font in italic
ToolTip	A pop-up window to provide some information about the control which the mouse pointer is held over it
Visible	The control is visible

The following subsections will examine the properties listed in Table 8.1 that we have not yet examined when describing the **textbox, label** and **button** controls in the previous chapter. You may assume that properties for the **checkboxlist** and other later controls operate the same way as described previously unless we explicitly state otherwise.

Items(x).Text

The **Items(x).Text** property allows you to change the text associated with each **checkbox** item. An example of its use is given below with a modified version of our previous fruits **checkbox** list script:

```
<%@Page Explicit="True" Language="VB" Strict="True" Debug="True" %>
<html>
    <head>
    <title>chapt8-2.aspx Checkboxes with .Text</title>
    </head>

    <script runat="server">
        Sub checkAnswer(Sender As Object, E As EventArgs)
            Dim intAnswers As Integer
            If fruits.Items(0).Selected = True
                intAnswers+=1
                fruits.Items(0).Text = "Orange - correct"
            End If
            If fruits.Items(1).Selected = True
                intAnswers-=1
            End If
            If fruits.Items(2).Selected = True
                intAnswers+=1
                fruits.Items(2).Text = "Plum - correct"
            End If
            If fruits.Items(3).Selected = True
                intAnswers+=1
                fruits.Items(3).Text = "Apple - correct"
            End If
            If fruits.Items(4).Selected = True
                intAnswers-=1
            End If
            If intAnswers = 3
```

```
                    answer.text = "Correct"
            Else
                    answer.text = "Wrong!"
            End If
        End Sub
    </script>

    <body>
    <form runat="server">
    Which of these are fruits?<br>
    <asp:checkboxlist id="fruits" runat="server">
            <asp:listitem>Orange</asp:listitem>
            <asp:listitem>Potato</asp:listitem>
            <asp:listitem>Plum</asp:listitem>
            <asp:listitem>Apple</asp:listitem>
            <asp:listitem>Cabbage</asp:listitem>
    </asp:checkboxlist>
    <br><asp:label id="answer" runat="server"/>
    <br><asp:button id="select" text="Check Answer" onclick="checkAnswer"
runat="server"/>
    </form>
    </body>
</html>
```

The above script uses the Items(x).Text property to alter the value of the item **text** so that if the correct checkbox item is selected the user is informed, for example:

```
fruits.Items(0).Text = "Orange - correct"
```

Items(x).Value

The Items(x).Value property allows you to examine or change the value associated with a listitem. Values can be set along with the listitem using the following syntax:

```
<asp:listitem value="string">ItemString</asp:listitem>
```

The value of the item can be accessed using the following syntax:

```
strVab = listname.Items(x).value
```

An example of using this property is introduced later in this chapter in the sections on drop-down lists and list boxes.

Items.Count

The Items.Count property allows you to determine the number of listitems there are currently. The syntax of this property is:

```
intVab = listname.Items.Count
```

An example of using this property is introduced later in this chapter in the section on list boxes.

Items.Add

The Items.Add property allows you to add a new listitem to the end of the current list. The syntax of this property is:

```
Listname.Items.Add(strName)
```

where strName is the text that you wish to appear as the listitem. An example of the use of this property appears in the manipulation list-items section of this chapter.

Items.Insert

The Items.Insert property allows you to insert a new listitem into the current list. The syntax of this property is:

```
Listname.Items.insert(x,strName)
```

where strName is the text that you wish to appear as the listitem and x is the position in the list where you wish to insert it. An example of the use of this property appears in the manipulation list-items section of this chapter.

Items.Remove

The Items.Remove property allows you to remove a listitem from the current list. The syntax of this property is:

Listname.Items.Remove(strName)

where strName is the name of the listitem you wish to remove. An example of the use of this property again appears in the manipulation list-items section of this chapter.

Items.RemoveAt

The Items.RemoveAt property allows you to remove a listitem at a specific position from the current list. The syntax of this property is:

Listname.Items.RemoveAt(x)

where x is the listitem position number that you wish to remove.

Items.Clear

The Items.Clear property allows you to remove all listitems from the current list. The syntax of this property is:

Listname.Items.Clear

An example of the use of this property appears in the manipulation list-items section of this chapter.

TextAlign

The TextAlign property allows you to determine if the text appears to the right or the left of the checkbox. The

following script illustrates two **checkboxlists,** one aligned
to the right and the other to the left:

```
<%@Page Explicit="True" Language="VB" Strict="True" Debug="True" %>
<html>
    <head>
    <title>chapt8-3.aspx Checkboxes TextAlign</title>
    </head>

    <body>
    <form runat="server">
    Right aligned fruits:<br>
    <asp:checkboxlist id="rfruits" textalign="right" runat="server">
        <asp:listitem>Orange</asp:listitem>
        <asp:listitem>Potato</asp:listitem>
        <asp:listitem>Plum</asp:listitem>
        <asp:listitem>Cabbage</asp:listitem>
    </asp:checkboxlist>
    Left aligned fruits:<br>
    <asp:checkboxlist id="lfruits" textalign="left" runat="server">
        <asp:listitem>Orange</asp:listitem>
        <asp:listitem>Potato</asp:listitem>
        <asp:listitem>Plum</asp:listitem>
        <asp:listitem>Cabbage</asp:listitem>
    </asp:checkboxlist>
    </form>
    </body>
</html>
```

Figure 8.2 illustrates the output from the above script. The
first **checkboxlist** uses the following syntax to align the text
to the right of the boxes:

```
<asp:checkboxlist id="rfruits" textalign="right" runat="server">
    <asp:listitem>Orange</asp:listitem>
    <asp:listitem>Potato</asp:listitem>
    <asp:listitem>Plum</asp:listitem>
    <asp:listitem>Cabbage</asp:listitem>
</asp:checkboxlist>
```

The second **checkboxlist** uses the syntax:

```
<asp:checkboxlist id="lfruits" textalign="left" runat="server">
    <asp:listitem>Orange</asp:listitem>
```

```
<asp:listitem>Potato</asp:listitem>
<asp:listitem>Plum</asp:listitem>
<asp:listitem>Cabbage</asp:listitem>
</asp:checkboxlist>
```

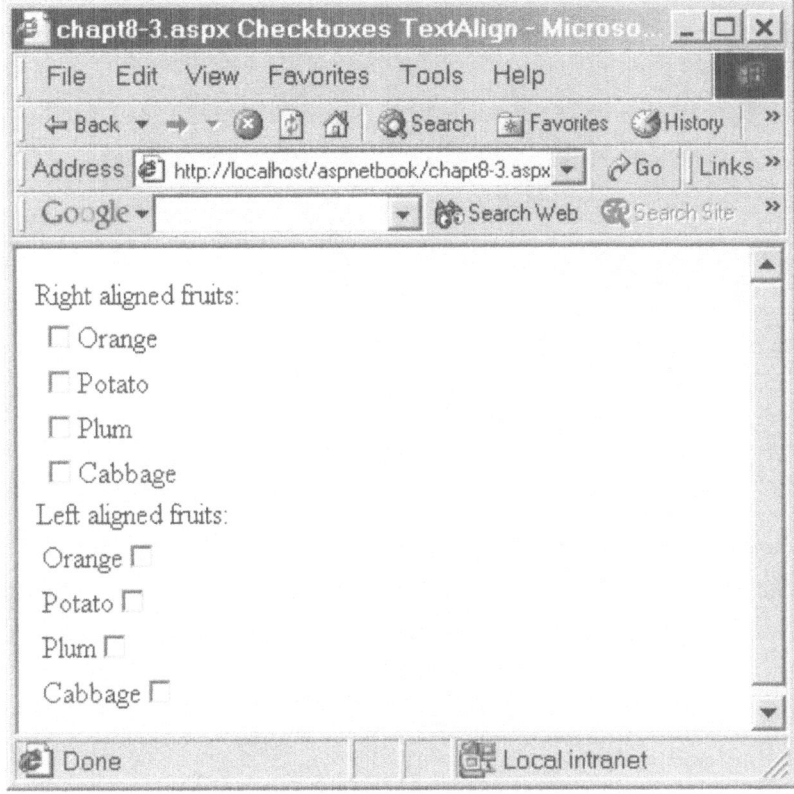

Figure 8.2 TextAlign

CellPadding and CellSpacing

When formatting a **checkboxlist** the server actually puts the individual checkboxes and text into separate invisible table cells. **CellPadding** specifies the space between the checkbox and the edge of the table cell. **CellSpacing** specifies the space between one cell and another. However, as you cannot see the table cells, both of these properties simply appear to move the checkboxes further apart. Consider the following example:

```
<%@Page Explicit="True" Language="VB" Strict="True" Debug="True" %>
<html>
    <head>
    <title>chapt8-4.aspx Checkboxes Cellspacing and Cellpadding</title>
    </head>

    <body>
    <form runat="server">
    Right aligned fruits:<br>
    <asp:checkboxlist id="rfruits" cellspacing="1" textalign="right" runat="server">
        <asp:listitem>Orange</asp:listitem>
        <asp:listitem>Potato</asp:listitem>
        <asp:listitem>Plum</asp:listitem>
        <asp:listitem>Cabbage</asp:listitem>
    </asp:checkboxlist>
    Left aligned fruits:<br>
    <asp:checkboxlist id="lfruits" cellpadding="6" textalign="left" runat="server">
        <asp:listitem>Orange</asp:listitem>
        <asp:listitem>Potato</asp:listitem>
        <asp:listitem>Plum</asp:listitem>
        <asp:listitem>Cabbage</asp:listitem>
    </asp:checkboxlist>
    </form>
    </body>
</html>
```

The above script produces two **checkboxlists** which illustrate **cellpadding** and **cellspacing**. In the first list a **cellspacing** of 1 is specified and in the second list a **cellpadding** of 6.

The output from this script is shown in Figure 8.3. Notice the different spacing between the two lists. Although the first and second lists are aligned differently it should be clear that there is far more space between the separate checkbox entries on the second list than on the first. Try adjusting the size of the **cellpadding** and **cellspacing** properties to see what different effects you can make.

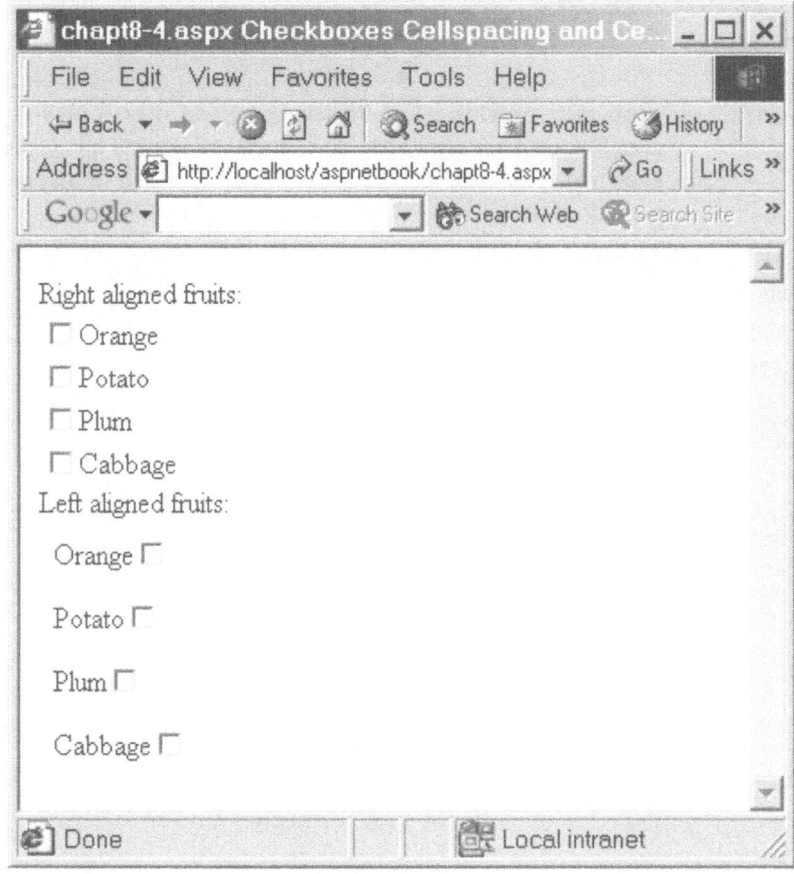

Figure 8.3 *Different cellspacing and cellpadding*

RepeatColumns, RepeatDirection and RepeatLayout

The RepeatColumns, RepeatDirection and RepeatLayout properties provide you with some control over how your checkboxlist should look. The RepeatColumns property specifies the number of columns, which are used to display your checkboxlist. For example:

```
<%@Page Explicit="True" Language="VB" Strict="True" Debug="True" %>
<html>
     <head>
     <title>chapt8-5.aspx Checkboxes repeatcolumns</title>
     </head>
     <body>
     <form runat="server">
     Right aligned fruits:<br>
     <asp:checkboxlist id="rfruits" repeatColumns="3" textalign="right"
runat="server">
          <asp:listitem>1. Orange</asp:listitem>
          <asp:listitem>2. Potato</asp:listitem>
          <asp:listitem>3. Plum</asp:listitem>
          <asp:listitem>4. Cabbage</asp:listitem>
          <asp:listitem>5. Apple</asp:listitem>
          <asp:listitem>6. Banana</asp:listitem>
          <asp:listitem>7. Carrot</asp:listitem>
          <asp:listitem>8. Lettuce</asp:listitem>
          <asp:listitem>9. Cherry</asp:listitem>
     </asp:checkboxlist>
     </form>
     </body>
</html>
```

This script produces a checkboxlist of three columns across the screen. The output from the above script is shown in Figure 8.4. Notice that the checkboxitems are displayed down each column from left to right. This is known as vertical direction and it is the default setting. If however the value of repeatDirection is set so that it has the value "horizontal" then the output listboxes are displayed across the columns, illustrated in Figure 8.5:

```
<asp:checkboxlist id="rfruits" repeatColumns="3" repeatDirection="horizontal" textalign="right" runat="server">
```

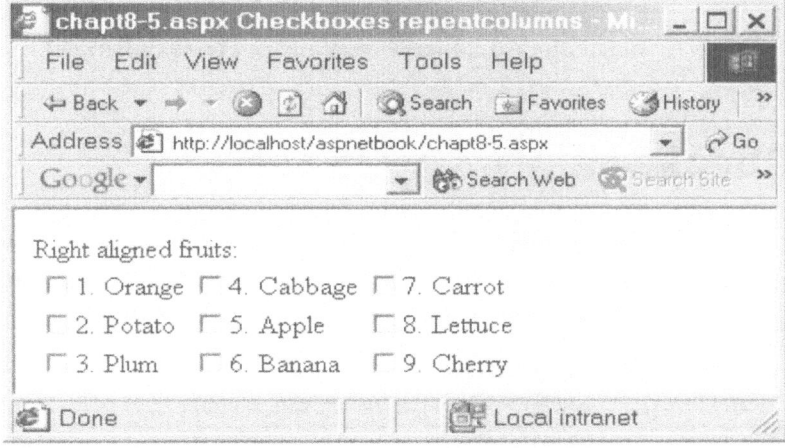

Figure 8.4 RepeatColumns checkboxlist

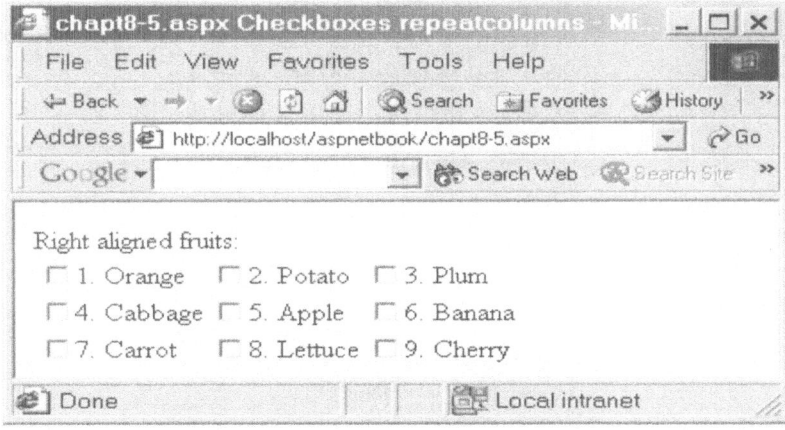

Figure 8.5 RepeatColumns checkboxlist with horizontal repeatDirection

AutoPostBack

The AutoPostBack property works exactly the same way as we illustrated for the textbox option. However, to detect that a change has occurred you need to use the SelectedIndexChanged event and not onTextChanged.

Checkbox

The checkbox control allows you to create single checkboxes and not lists of them. Table 8.2 lists the properties that we can use with the checkbox control.

Table 8.2 Checkbox properties

Property	Description
TextAlign	Whether the text appears to the left or right of the checkbox
Text	The text appearing by the checkbox
Checked	Whether a checkmark appears in the checkbox
AutoPostBack	The page should return to the server when the checkbox is modified
BackColor	The background colour of the control
BorderColor	The border colour of the control
BorderStyle	The style of the border surrounding the control
Enabled	The control is enabled
ForeColor	The colour of the text string
Height	Height of the control
Width	Width of the control
Font-Name	Font typeface
Font-Size	Size of the text displayed
Font-Bold	Font is bold
Font-Underline	Font is underlined
Font-Italic	Font in italic
ToolTip	A pop-up window to provide some information about the control which the mouse pointer is held over it
Visible	The control is visible

Text

The following script provides an example of the **checkbox** control and the **Text** property:

```
<%@Page Explicit="True" Language="VB" Strict="True" Debug="True" %>
<html>
    <head>
    <title>chapt8-6.aspx Checkbox</title>
    </head>

    <body>
    <form runat="server">
    Two final questions:<br>
    <asp:checkbox id="question1" text="Don't send me any information"
textalign="right" runat="server"/>
    <br>
    <asp:checkbox id="question2" text="Please send me some information"
checked="true" textalign="right" runat="server"/>
    </form>
    </body>
</html>
```

The output from the above script is shown in Figure 8.6.

Checked

In the case of single checkboxes we use the **Checked** property to determine if the **checkbox** has been checked or not, as opposed to the **checkboxlist** where we use the **item(x).selected** property. The checked property returns a Boolean value of true or false depending on whether it is checked or not. The syntax of using this property to see if a **checkbox** is checked is:

```
If checkboxname.Checked = True
```

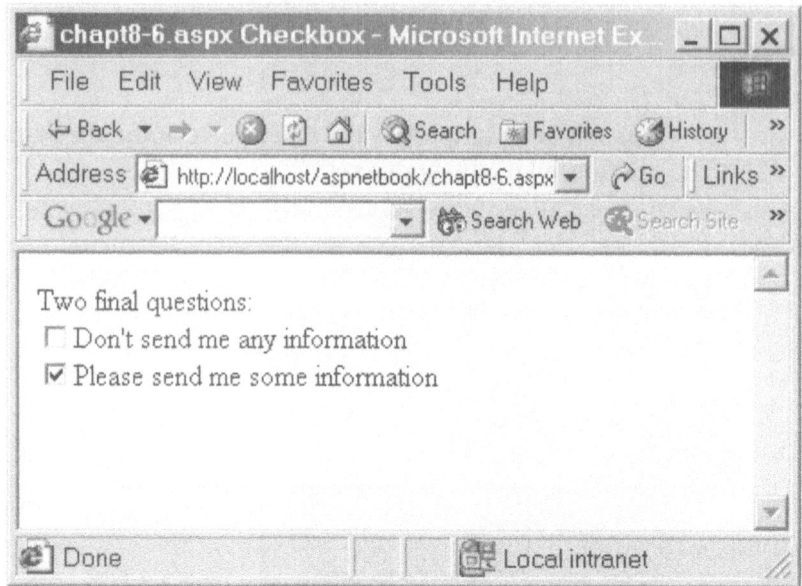

Figure 8.6 Single Checkbox controls

AutoPostBack

The AutoPostBack property works exactly the same way as we illustrated for the **textbox** option. However, to detect that a change has occurred you need to use the onCheckChanged event and not onTextChanged.

RadioButtonLists

Radio button lists are similar to checkbox lists but instead of allowing multiple items to be selected, radio buttons allow only one. The syntax for the control is as follows:

```
<asp:radiobuttonlist id="name" runat="server">
```

```
<asp:listitem>ItemDescription</asp:listitem>
  :

  :

</asp:radiobuttonlist>
```

The **radiobuttonlist** control surrounds a number of **listitem** controls. There is one **listitem** control for each radio button. Consider the following example script:

```
<%@Page Explicit="True" Language="VB" Strict="True" Debug="True" %>
<html>
    <head>
    <title>chapt8-7.aspx RadioButtonList</title>
    </head>

    <script runat="server">
        Sub checkAnswer(Sender As Object, E As EventArgs)
            If q1.Items(2).Selected = True Then

                answer.text = "Correct"
            Else
                answer.text = "Wrong!"
            End If
        End Sub
    </script>

    <body>
    <form runat="server">
    Q1. What is the value of 5 x 3?<br>
    <asp:radiobuttonlist id="q1" runat="server">
        <asp:listitem>13</asp:listitem>
        <asp:listitem>14</asp:listitem>
        <asp:listitem>15</asp:listitem>
        <asp:listitem>16</asp:listitem>
        <asp:listitem>17</asp:listitem>
    </asp:radiobuttonlist>
    <br><asp:label id="answer" runat="server"/>
    <br><asp:button id="select" text="Check Answer" onclick="checkAnswer"
runat="server"/>
    </form>
    </body>
</html>
```

The output from the above script is shown in Figure 8.7.

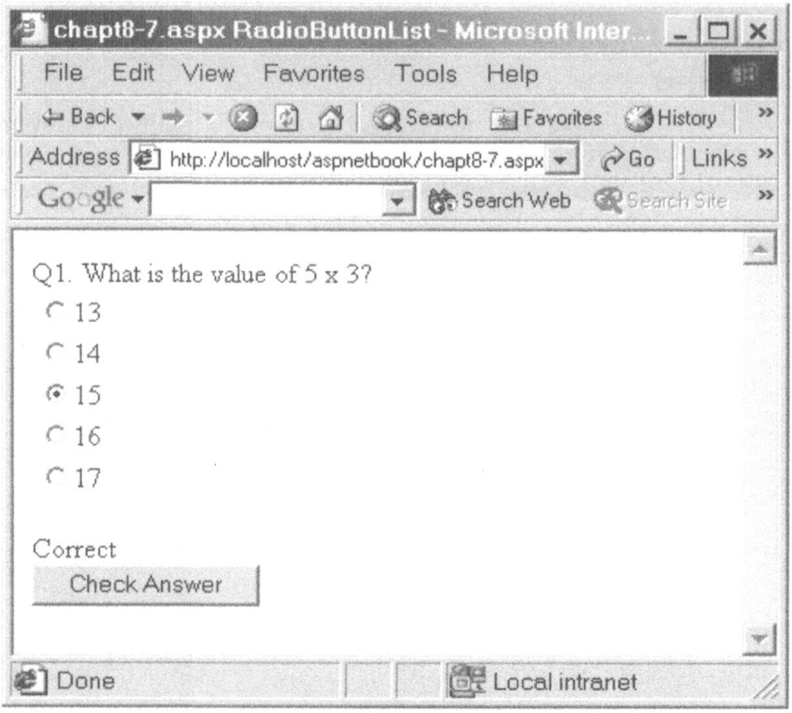

Figure 8.7 *RadioButtonList*

The above script includes a simple **radiobuttonlist**:

```
<asp:radiobuttonlist id="q1" runat="server">
    <asp:listitem>13</asp:listitem>
    <asp:listitem>14</asp:listitem>
    <asp:listitem>15</asp:listitem>
    <asp:listitem>16</asp:listitem>
    <asp:listitem>17</asp:listitem>
</asp:radiobuttonlist>
```

When the check answer button is clicked the subroutine **checkAnswer** examines the value of **q1.Items(2).Selected** to see if this is set to True. If so then the text of the form label is set to **"Correct!"**.

Table 8.3 lists the properties that work with the radiobuttonlist.

Table 8.3 RadioButtonList control properties

Property	Description
Items(x).Selected	A boolean value indicating if the radiobuttonitem has been selected
Items(x).Text	The text which is used to label the radiobutton item
Items(x).Value	The value associated with this item
Items.Add(String)	Add a new item to the end of the list
Items.Insert(x, String)	Insert a new item at position x
Items.Remove(String)	Remove item from the list
Items.Clear	Removes all items from the list
Items.Count	Count the number of items in the list
Items.RemoveAt(x)	Remove the list item at position X
AutoPostBack	The page should return to the server when the radiobutton has been modified
CellPadding	The space around the radiobutton and the table cell
CellSpacing	The space between each table cell
TextAlign	Whether the text appears to the left or right of the radiobutton
RepeatColumns	Number of columns used to display the radio button
RepeatDirection	The direction on the page that the radio buttons are displayed
RepeatLayout	Uses a HTML table to neatly display the radio buttons
BackColor	The background colour of the control
BorderColor	The border colour of the control
BorderStyle	The style of the border surrounding the control
Enabled	The control is enabled
ForeColor	The colour of the text string
Height	Height of the control
Width	Width of the control
Font-Name	Font typeface
Font-Size	Size of the text displayed
Font-Bold	Font is bold
Font-Underline	Font is underlined
Font-Italic	Font in italic
ToolTip	A pop-up window to provide some information about the control which the mouse pointer is held over it
Visible	The control is visible
SelectedIndex	A number indicating what radio button has been selected
SelectedItem	The text of the radio button selected

SelectedIndex and SelectedItem.Text

The SelectedIndex and SelectedItem.Text properties are new to the RadioButtonList. The following script illustrates an example of using these properties:

```
<%@Page Explicit="True" Language="VB" Strict="True" Debug="True" %>
<html>
    <head>
    <title>chapt8-8.aspx RadioButtonList SelectedIndex and SelectedItem</title>
    </head>
    <script runat="server">
            Sub checkAnswer(Sender As Object, E As EventArgs)
                If q1.SelectedItem.Text = "15" Then
                    answer.text = "Correct"
                End If
                If q1.SelectedIndex <> 2 Then
                    answer.text = "Wrong!"
                End If
            End Sub
    </script>
    <body>
    <form runat="server">
    Q1. What is the value of 5 x 3?<br>
    <asp:radiobuttonlist id="q1" runat="server">
            <asp:listitem>13</asp:listitem>
            <asp:listitem>14</asp:listitem>
            <asp:listitem>15</asp:listitem>
            <asp:listitem>16</asp:listitem>
            <asp:listitem>17</asp:listitem>
    </asp:radiobuttonlist>
    <br><asp:label id="answer" runat="server"/>
    <br><asp:button id="select" text="Check Answer" onclick="checkAnswer"
runat="server"/>
    </form>
    </body>
</html>
```

The SelectedItem.Text property allows us to determine if the item selected from the list is equal to a certain value:

```
If q1.SelectedItem.Text = "15" Then
        answer.text = "Correct"
```

The **SelectedIndex** allows us to determine if a particular **listitem** number was selected, for example:

```
If q1.SelectedIndex <> 2 Then
        answer.text = "Wrong!"
```

AutoPostBack

The **AutoPostBack** property works exactly the same way as we illustrated for the checkbox control in that you need to use the **onCheckChanged** event.

RadioButton

Just like checkboxes, individual radio buttons can be created. These can be positioned in different parts of the web page, but can still link to one another using the **GroupName** property.

Table 8.4 lists the available properties.

Groupname

While you are able to create individual buttons on a form you may require some of these to be able to operate together. This is accomplished through the use of the **Groupname** property.

Table 8.4 Radiobutton properties

Property	Description
TextAlign	Whether the text appears to the left or right of the radiobutton
Checked	Whether a checkmark appears in the radiobutton
AutoPostBack	Page should return to the server if the radiobutton has been modified
BackColor	The background colour of the control
BorderColor	The border colour of the control
BorderStyle	The style of the border surrounding the control
Enabled	The control is enabled
ForeColor	The colour of the text string
Height	Height of the control
Width	Width of the control
Font-Name	Font typeface
Font-Size	Size of the text displayed
Font-Bold	Font is bold
Font-Underline	Font is underlined
Font-Italic	Font in italic
ToolTip	A pop-up window to provide some information about the control which the mouse pointer is held over it
Visible	The control is visible
Groupname	Groups together various buttons on a page

The following script illustrates the use of the **radiobutton** control using the **Groupname** property:

```
<%@Page Explicit="True" Language="VB" Strict="True" Debug="True" %>
<html>
    <head>
    <title>chapt8-9.aspx RadioButton Control</title>
    </head>

    <script runat="server">
        Sub checkAnswer(Sender As Object, E As EventArgs)
            If a3.checked = True Then
                answer.text = "Correct"
            Else
                answer.text = "Wrong!"
            End If
        End Sub
    </script>
    <body>
    <form runat="server">
    Q1. What is the value of 5 x 3?<br>
```

```
<asp:radiobutton id="a1" runat="server" text="13" groupname="Q1"/>
<asp:radiobutton id="a2" runat="server" text="14" groupname="Q1"/>
<asp:radiobutton id="a3" runat="server" text="15" groupname="Q1"/>
<asp:radiobutton id="a4" runat="server" text="16" groupname="Q1"/>
<asp:radiobutton id="a5" runat="server" text="17" groupname="Q1"/>
<br><asp:label id="answer" runat="server"/>
<br><asp:button id="select" text="Check Answer" onclick="checkAnswer"
runat="server"/>
</form>
</body>
</html>
```

The above script uses the **radiobutton** control to produce the same functionality as the previous **radiobuttonlist** control example. Notice that the buttons in this example are displayed across the web page and not down, see Figure 8.8. This is because each **radiobutton** control is separate and we have not included a <br> element to force them to be displayed on a separate line.

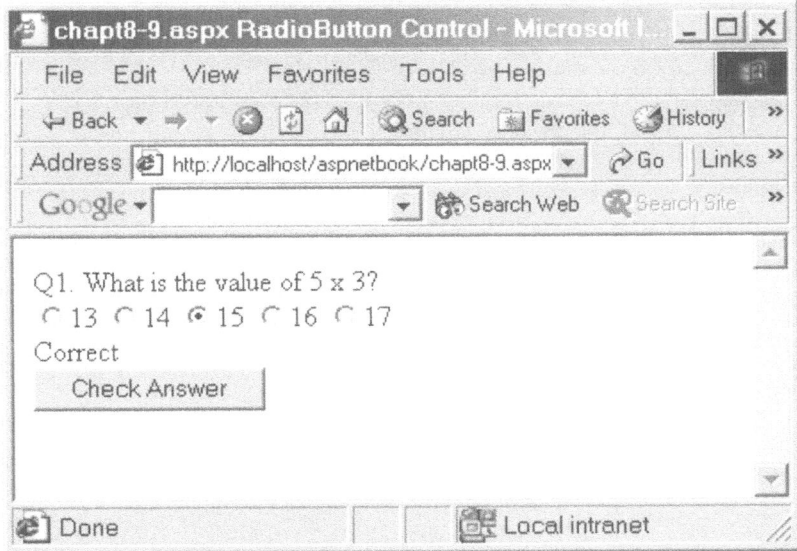

Figure 8.8 Individual radiobuttons

DropDownList

The DropDownList is a cross between a **textbox** and a **button**. When you click on the DropDownList button a list of options appears allowing you to select one. The option selected is then displayed. Table 8.5 lists the various properties that are supported.

Table 8.5 DropDownList control properties

Property	Description
Items(x).Selected	A boolean value indicating if the dropdownlist item has been selected
Items(x).Text	The text which is used to label the dropdownlist item
Items(x).Value	The value associated with this item
Items.Add(String)	Add a new item to the end of the list
Items.Insert(x, String)	Insert a new item at position x
Items.Remove(String)	Remove item from the list
Items.Clear	Removes all items from the list
Items.Count	Count the number of items in the list
Items.RemoveAt(x)	Remove the list item at position X
AutoPostBack	Page should return to the server if the dropdown has been modified
BackColor	The background colour of the control
BorderColor	The border colour of the control
BorderStyle	The style of the border surrounding the control
Enabled	The control is enabled
ForeColor	The colour of the text string
Height	Height of the control
Width	Width of the control
Font-Name	Font typeface
Font-Size	Size of the text displayed
Font-Bold	Font is bold
Font-Underline	Font is underlined
Font-Italic	Font in italic
ToolTip	A pop-up window to provide some information about the control which the mouse pointer is held over it
Visible	The control is visible
SelectedIndex	A number indicating what dropdownlist item has been selected
SelectedItem	The text of the dropdownlist item selected

Dropdown lists can be used to provide a very neat user interface design, allowing a large amount of information to be presented on the web page in a relatively small amount of space.

The following script provides an example of the use of the **DropDownList** control:

```
<%@Page Explicit="True" Language="VB" Strict="True" Debug="True" %>
<html>
      <head>
      <title>chapt8-10.aspx Drop Down List Control</title>
      </head>
      <script runat="server">
            Sub listprocess(Sender As Object, E As EventArgs)
                  If IsPostBack = False
                        answer.text = ""
                  End If
                  If cars.Items(0).Selected = True
                        answer.text = ""
                  Else
                        answer.text = "The cost of this car is £" &
cars.Items(cars.SelectedIndex).value
                  End If
            End Sub
      </script>
      <body>
      Please select which car you would like to buy!
      <form runat="server">
      <asp:dropdownlist id="cars" runat="server" autopostback="true"
onselectedindexchanged="listprocess">
            <asp:listitem></asp:listitem>
            <asp:listitem value="5,500">Ford Ka</asp:listitem>
            <asp:listitem value="10,500">Mazda 323</asp:listitem>
            <asp:listitem value="7,500">Nissan Micra</asp:listitem>
            <asp:listitem value="15,500">Vauxhall Vectra</asp:listitem>
            <asp:listitem value="29,500">BMW 330i</asp:listitem>
      </asp:dropdownlist>
      <br><asp:label id="answer" runat="server"/>
      </form>
      </body>
</html>
```

The above script uses an **AutoPostBack** event to trigger the return to the server and the invocation of subroutine **listprocess**:

```
<asp:dropdownlist id="cars" runat="server" autopostback="true"
onselectedindexchanged="listprocess">
```

In the subroutine **listprocess** the value associated with the selected item is displayed as **labeltext**:

```
answer.text = "The cost of this car is £" & cars.Items(cars.SelectedIndex).value
```

This results in the value of the selected car being displayed each time the different drop down menu item is selected.

The output from this script is shown in Figure 8.9.

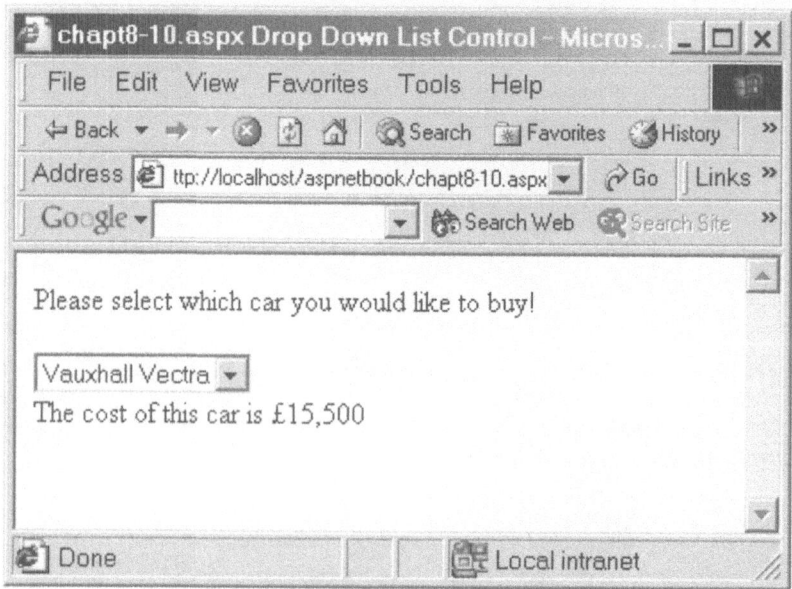

Figure 8.9 Dropdown list

ListBox

A ListBox allows the user to select a number of items from a long list, its properties are listed in Table 8.6.

Table 8.6 ListBox control properties

Property	Description
Items(x).Selected	A boolean value indicating if the listbox item has been selected
Items(x).Text	The text which is used to label the listbox item
Items(x).Value	The value associated with this item
Items.Add(String)	Add a new item to the end of the list
Items.Insert(x, String)	Insert a new item at position x.
Items.Remove(String)	Remove item from the list
Items.Clear	Removes all items from the list
Items.Count	Count the number of items in the list
Items.RemoveAt(x)	Remove the list item at position X
AutoPostBack	Page should return to the server when the textbox has been modified
SelectionMode	Indicates if the user can select one or multiple items from the listbox
BackColor	The background colour of the control
BorderColor	The border colour of the control
BorderStyle	The style of the border surrounding the control
Enabled	The control is enabled
ForeColor	The colour of the text string
Height	Height of the control
Width	Width of the control
Font-Name	Font typeface
Font-Size	Size of the text displayed
Font-Bold	Font is bold
Font-Underline	Font is underlined
Font-Italic	Font in italic
ToolTip	A pop-up window to provide some information about the control which the mouse pointer is held over it
Visible	The control is visible
SelectedIndex	A number indicating what dropdownlist item has been selected
SelectedItem	The text of the dropdownlist item selected
Column	The width of the control in characters
Row	The height of the control in lines

The list is scrollable and can be set to show a certain number of list items on the web page.

SelectionMode

The **SelectionMode** property allows a user to select single or multiple items from a **listbox** control. The property can be set to the values **"multiple"** or **"single"**. The following script illustrates an example of a list box:

```
<%@Page Explicit="True" Language="VB" Strict="True" Debug="True" %>
<html>
    <head>
    <title>chapt8-11.aspx ListBox Control</title>
    </head>
    <script runat="server">
        Sub listprocess(Sender As Object, E As EventArgs)
            Dim intItemCount As Integer
            Dim intTotalCost As Integer = 0

            For intItemCount = 0 To cars.Items.Count - 1
                If cars.Items(intItemCount).Selected
                    intTotalCost += Cint(cars.Items(intItemCount).Value)
                End If
            Next
            If intTotalCost <> 0 Then
                answer.text = "The cost of these cars is £" & CStr(intTotalCost)
            Else
                answer.text = ""
            End If
        End Sub
    </script>
    <body>
    Please select which cars you would like to buy!
    <form runat="server">
    <asp:listbox id="cars" runat="server" selectionmode="multiple"
autopostback="true" onselectedindexchanged="listprocess">
        <asp:listitem value="5500">Ford Ka</asp:listitem>
        <asp:listitem value="10500">Mazda 323</asp:listitem>
        <asp:listitem value="7500">Nissan Micra</asp:listitem>
        <asp:listitem value="15500">Vauxhall Vectra</asp:listitem>
```

```
        <asp:listitem value="29500">BMW 330i</asp:listitem>
    </asp:listbox>
    <br><asp:label id="answer" runat="server"/>
    </form>
    </body>
</html>
```

The above script is a modification of our previous DropDownList example. However, here the user can select more than one vehicle to purchase. Inside the listprocess subroutine a For loop is used to access each listitem to see if this has been selected and if so the value stored in the Value property is added to variable intTotalCost:

```
For intItemCount = 0 To cars.Items.Count - 1
    If cars.Items(intItemCount).Selected
        intTotalCost += Cint(cars.Items(intItemCount).Value)
    End If
Next
```

The output from this script is shown in Figure 8.10.

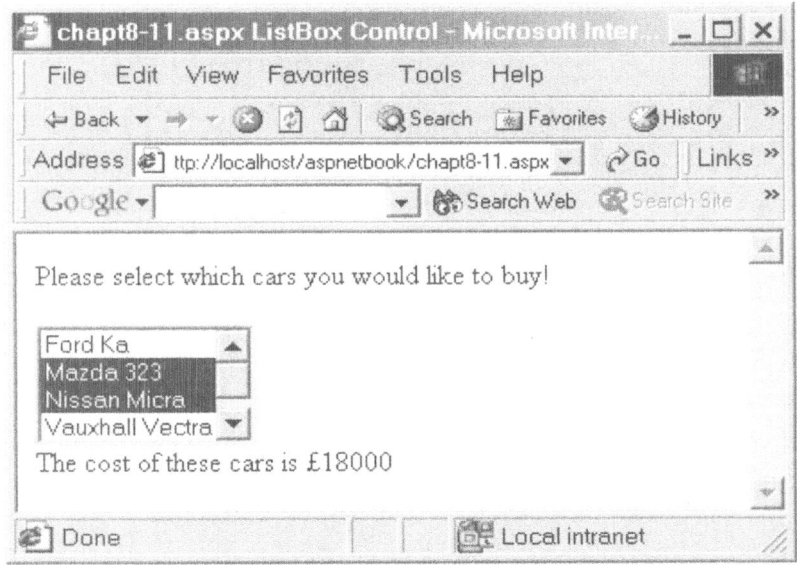

Figure 8.10 Multiple selection of listbox items

Manipulating ListItems

A variety of different properties for adding, deleting and inserting list items were introduced previously.

The following script illustrates how they can dynamically effect and change the property of a list:

```
<%@Page Explicit="True" Language="VB" Strict="True" Debug="True" %>
<html>
    <head>
    <title>chapt8-12.aspx Controlling Items in a list</title>
    </head>

    <script runat="server">
        Sub listprocess(Sender As Object, E As EventArgs)
            If IsPostBack = False
                answer.text = ""
            End If
            If cars.Items(0).Selected = True
                answer.text = ""
            Else
                answer.text = "The cost of this car is £" &
cars.Items(cars.SelectedIndex).value
            End If
        End Sub

        Sub addCar(Sender As Object, E As EventArgs)
            Dim intItemCount As Integer
            intItemCount = cars.Items.Count-1
            If newpos.text = "" Then
                cars.Items.Add(newcar.text)
                cars.Items(intItemCount).Value = newvalue.text

            Else
                cars.Items.Insert(Cint(newpos.text),newcar.text)

                cars.Items(Cint(newpos.text)).Value = newvalue.text

            End If
            newcar.text=""
```

```
                newvalue.text=""
                newpos.text=""
        End Sub

        Sub deleteCar(Sender As Object, E As EventArgs)
                response.write(newcar.text)
                cars.Items.Remove(cars.SelectedItem)
                newcar.text=""
                newvalue.text=""
        End Sub

        Sub clearCar(Sender As Object, E As EventArgs)
                cars.Items.Clear
                newcar.text=""
                newvalue.text=""
        End Sub
    </script>

    <body>
    Please select which car you would like to buy!
    <form runat="server">
    <asp:dropdownlist id="cars" runat="server" autopostback="true"
onselectedindexchanged="listprocess">
            <asp:listitem></asp:listitem>
            <asp:listitem value="5,500">Ford Ka</asp:listitem>
            <asp:listitem value="10,500">Mazda 323</asp:listitem>
            <asp:listitem value="7,500">Nissan Micra</asp:listitem>
            <asp:listitem value="15,500">Vauxhall Vectra</asp:listitem>
            <asp:listitem value="29,500">BMW 330i</asp:listitem>
    </asp:dropdownlist>
    <br><asp:label id="answer" runat="server"/>
    <br><br><br>Car:<asp:textbox id="newcar" runat="server"/>
    <br>Value:<asp:textbox id="newvalue" runat="server"/>
    <br>Position:<asp:textbox id="newpos" runat="server"/>
    <br><asp:button onclick="addCar" text="Add Car" runat="server"/>
    <br><asp:button onclick="deleteCar" text="Delete Car" runat="server"/>

    <br><asp:button onclick="clearCar" text="Clear All Cars" runat="server"/>

    </form>
    </body>
</html>
```

The above script is essentially the same as the dropdown menu script illustrated previously. This script however has been enhanced to provide you with the ability to add a car to the list, remove a car from the list, clear the list and insert a new car at a certain position on the list. The ASP.NET form controls are as follows:

```
<form runat="server">
<asp:dropdownlist id="cars" runat="server" autopostback="true"
onselectedindexchanged="listprocess">
    <asp:listitem></asp:listitem>
    <asp:listitem value="5,500">Ford Ka</asp:listitem>
    <asp:listitem value="10,500">Mazda 323</asp:listitem>
    <asp:listitem value="7,500">Nissan Micra</asp:listitem>
    <asp:listitem value="15,500">Vauxhall Vectra</asp:listitem>
    <asp:listitem value="29,500">BMW 330i</asp:listitem>
</asp:dropdownlist>
<br><asp:label id="answer" runat="server"/>
<br><br><br>Car:<asp:textbox id="newcar" runat="server"/>
<br>Value:<asp:textbox id="newvalue" runat="server"/>
<br>Position:<asp:textbox id="newpos" runat="server"/>
<br><asp:button onclick="addCar" text="Add Car" runat="server"/>
<br><asp:button onclick="deleteCar" text="Delete Car" runat="server"/>
<br><asp:button onclick="clearCar" text="Clear All Cars" runat="server"/>
</form>
```

The form introduces three textbox fields to allow the name, value and position of the car data to be added to the list to be entered. After typing a cars name, value and position in the list you wish it to appear, into the appropriate textboxes, clicking on the Add button results in the addCar subroutine being invoked:

```
Sub addCar(Sender As Object, E As EventArgs)
    Dim intItemCount As Integer
    intItemCount = cars.Items.Count-1
    If newpos.text = "" Then
        cars.Items.Add(newcar.text)
        cars.Items(intItemCount).Value = newvalue.text
    Else
        cars.Items.Insert(Cint(newpos.text),newcar.text)
        cars.Items(Cint(newpos.text)).Value = newvalue.text
    End If
```

```
                newcar.text=""
                newvalue.text=""
                newpos.text=""
        End Sub
```

This subroutine checks to see if any data has been entered into the position **textbox**. If so the new car is inserted into the list at that position. If nothing has been entered in the position **textbox** then the car is added to the end of the list. The value of the car is also stored along with its label, but no check is made to see if this has been added. Figure 8.11 illustrates the output from this script.

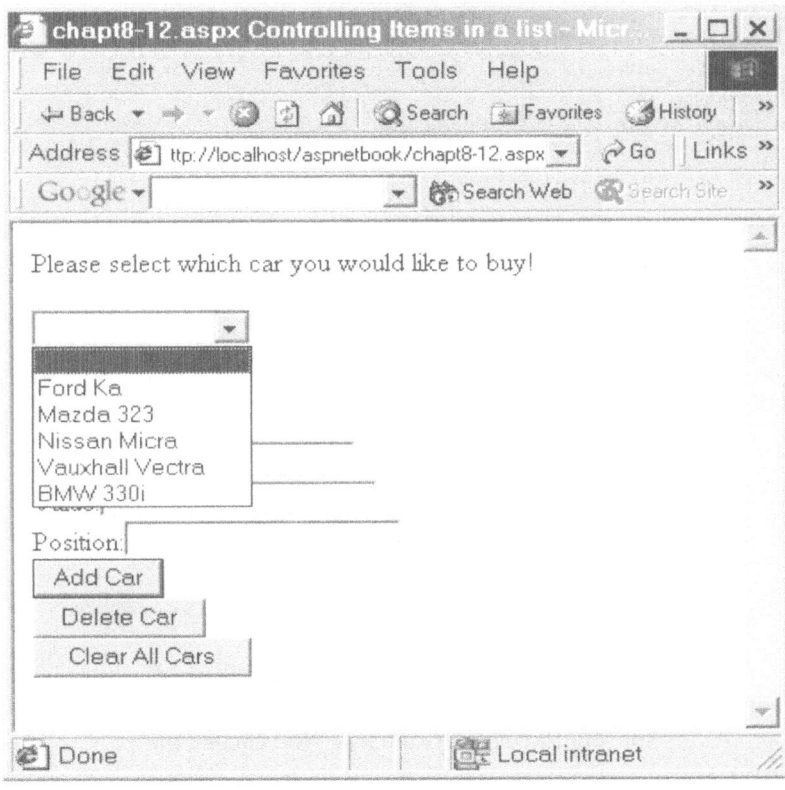

Figure 8.11 Adding, removing, inserting and clearing items

Clicking the Clear button will completely remove the contents of the list by invoking the **clearCar** subroutine. Selecting a car from the **DropDownList** and then clicking the Delete button will invoke the **deletecar** subroutine and remove the car from the list.

LinkButton

A **LinkButton** is a button, disguised as a hyperlink. Consider the following example:

```
<%@Page Explicit="True" Language="VB" Strict="True" Debug="True" %>
<html>
      <head>
      <title>chapt8-13.aspx LinkButton</title>
      </head>

      <script runat="server">
            Sub linkProcess(Sender As Object, E As EventArgs)
                  Response.Write("You clicked me!")
            End Sub
      </script>

      <body>
      <form runat="server">
      <asp:linkbutton id="link" runat="server" onclick="linkProcess">
      Click me
      </asp:linkbutton>
      </form>
      </body>
</html>
```

The above script employs a **LinkButton** which when clicked involves the subroutine called **linkProcess**. This subrountine displays the text *"You clicked me"*.

Summary

This chapter has introduced a variety of different ASP.NET form server controls. Each control has a large number of properties associated with it, some of which we have examined in this chapter. Hopefully you will now have some idea how to create ASP.NET server controls and use them to aid interaction between the user and the web page. In the following chapter we shall examine two additional controls.

Chapter
9

Calendar and Adrotator Controls

Introduction

This chapter introduces two special interface controls, the Calendar and Adrotator controls.

Calendar

The Calendar control is a very powerful and useful additional to the server controls available within ASP.NET. In its simplest form it is extremely easy to use as shown in the following script:

```
<%@Page Explicit="True" Language="VB" Strict="True" Debug="True" %>
<html>
    <head>
    <title>chapt9-1.aspx Calendar Control</title>
    </head>

    <body>
    <form runat="server">
    <asp:calendar id="thisMonth" runat="server"/>
    </form>
    </body>
</html>
```

The above script uses the basic Calendar control to produce a simple calendar on the web page. This is illustrated in Figure 9.1. Even with this simplest of scripts we can still interact with the Calendar control. If you click on any of the dates displayed on the Calendar you will see that this is highlighted (although nothing else happens as we haven't just written any code to capture this event). You can also scroll forward and backwards through the months of the year by clicking on the < and > characters to the left and right of the calendar month title.

We can display a neat calendar as part of an ASP.NET form, but what else can we do with this? Well consider

Table 9.1, which lists some of the many different properties of the calendar control that we can access.

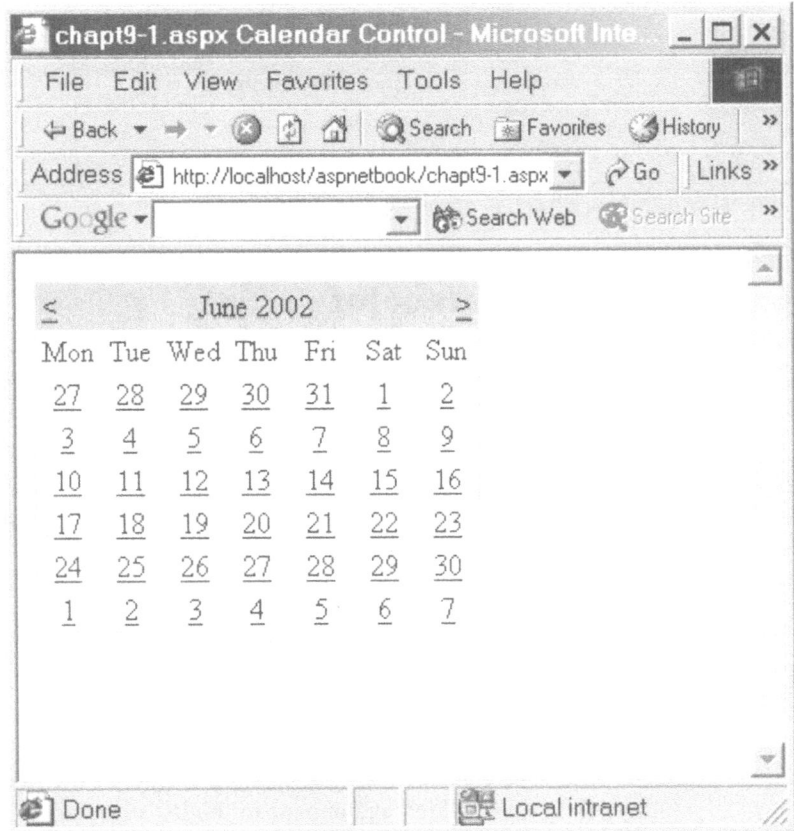

Figure 9.1 Calendar control

In actual fact the **Calendar** control has a large number of properties that can be used to affect the way it looks and operates. We do not have enough space to examine all of these in this book so we shall consider a small selection of these.

Table 9.1 Calendar properties

Property	Description
Onselectionchanged	Captures the event of the user clicking on the calendar control
Showgridlines	Whether gridlines are displayed
Firstdayofweek	Which day of the week is displayed on the calendar in the first column
VisibleDate	The date which is displayed on the calendar
BackColor	Background colour
ForeColor	Foreground text colour
Selecteddate	The date which has been selected by the user
Shownextprevmonth	Whether the next and previous month buttons are visible

Backcolor and Forecolor

Backcolor and Forecolor allow us to alter the colour of the calendar background and text colour. The colours that can be used are the same as those listed in Chapter 7. The syntax for use is:

```
Backcolor="colour"
Forecolor="colour"
```

Where "colour" is the colour you wish to use.

Firstdayofweek

The Firstdayofweek property allows you to specify the first day of the week, which will appear in the left most column of the calendar. The syntax is:

```
Firstdayofweek="day"
```

Showgridlines

The Showgridlines property allows you to specify if gridlines are displayed on the Calendar control separating the days of the month. The property takes a Boolean value of true or false and is set to false as a default.

Shownextprevmonth

This property allows you to disable the next and previous month buttons from the top of the control stopping the user scrolling backwards and forwards through the months. The control takes a Boolean true or false value and is set to true as a default.

Visibledate

This property allows you to specify the date that is displayed on the **Calendar** control. The syntax is as follows:

```
Visibledate="date"
```

Where **"date"** is the date to display. The following script is a modification of the previous example illustrating the different properties, which have just been discussed:

```
<%@Page Explicit="True" Language="VB" Strict="True" Debug="True" %>
<html>
    <head>
    <title>chapt9-2.aspx Calendar Control Properties</title>
    </head>
    <body>
    <form runat="server">
    <asp:calendar id="thisMonth"
    VisibleDate="01/01/2000"
    FirstDayOfWeek="Sunday"
    Shownextprevmonth="false"
    Showgridlines="true"
    forecolor="yellow"
    backcolor="blue"
    runat="server"/>
    </form>
    </body>
```

```
</html>
```

The output from the above script is illustrated in Figure 9.2. Notice that the gridlines are present and the previous and next buttons are missing. Also, notice that the date shown is the 1st January 2000 and the first day of the week is Sunday.

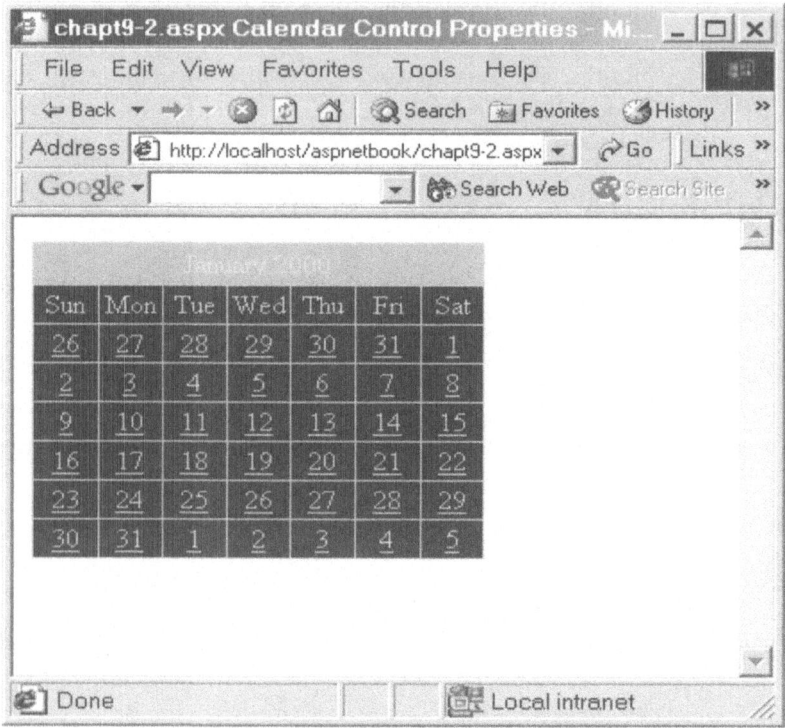

Figure 9.2 Calendar properties

Onselectionchanged and SelectedDate

The **Onselectionchanged** property allows us to capture a user's click as an event. The **SelectedDate** property allows us to access the date clicked by the user.

The following script provides an example of using these two properties:

```
<%@Page Explicit="True" Language="VB" Strict="True" Debug="True" %>
<html>
    <head>
    <title>chapt9-3.aspx Calendar Events</title>
    </head>

    <script runat="server">
        Sub processDate(Sender As Object, E As EventArgs)
        firstlabel.text = CStr(firstDate.SelectedDate)
        secondlabel.text = CStr(secondDate.SelectedDate)
        thirdlabel.text =
CStr(DateDiff("d",firstDate.SelectedDate,secondDate.SelectedDate))
        End Sub
    </script>

    <body>
    <form runat="server">
    <asp:calendar id="firstDate"
    runat="server" onselectionchanged="processDate"/>
    <asp:label id="firstlabel" runat="server"/>
    <br>
    <asp:calendar id="secondDate"
    runat="server" onselectionchanged="processDate"/>
    <asp:label id="secondlabel" runat="server"/>
    <br>Difference in days is <asp:label id="thirdlabel" runat="server"/>
    </form>
    </body>
</html>
```

The above script produces a form with two calendar controls and three labels. The output from this script is shown in Figure 9.3.

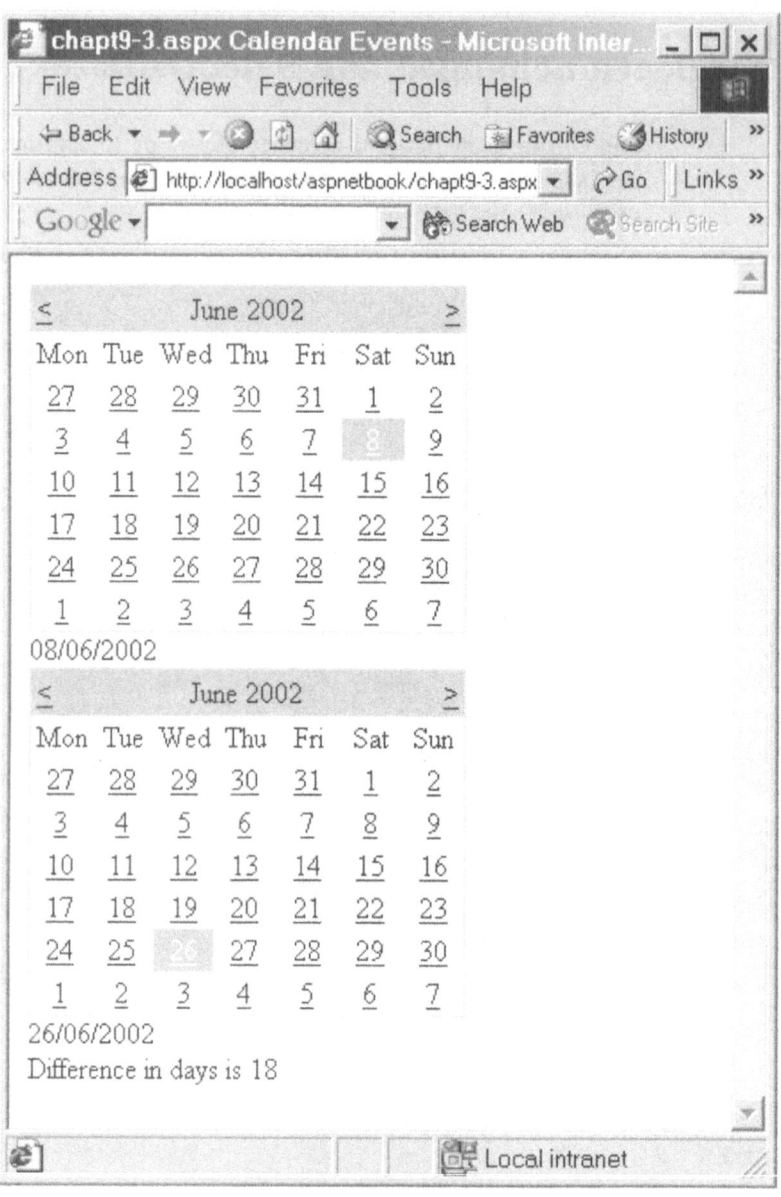

Figure 9.3 Calendar events

When the user selects a date from either calendar the date is displayed in one of the two labels below each calendar. In addition, the **DateDiff** function is used to calculate the difference in days between the two dates:

```
thirdlabel.text = CStr(DateDiff("d",firstDate.SelectedDate,secondDate.SelectedDate))
```

and this is also displayed.

Adrotator

The **Adrotator** control allows you to place different adverts on your page, the frequency of which you can control whenever the page is reloaded. The control is simple to use and has the following syntax:

```
<asp:adrotator id="Ad" runat="server" advertisementfile="file.xml"/>
```

Notice that the control has properties, the **runat="server"** property like all of our other controls and an **advertisementfile** control. This control points to an XML file which specified what and how our advert is going to operate. The following script illustrates the use of your **adrotator**, although don't run this yet as we still have some work to do:

```
<%@Page Explicit="True" Language="VB" Strict="True" Debug="True" %>
<html>
    <head>
    <title>chapt9-4.aspx Adrotator</title>
    </head>

    <body>
    <form runat="server">
    <asp:adrotator id="Ad" runat="server" advertisementfile="flower.xml"/>
    </form>
    </body>
</html>
```

The first thing we need to do is produce some graphics that can be used in our advert. We have produced three graphics for a flower shop and these are illustrated in Figure 9.4.

Figure 9.4 *Our advert graphics*

You will need to create some simple graphics of your own to continue. You can use the Paint tool that is included with Windows to create these. It doesn't matter what size you make them, or what graphics or text they include. Save the three files as JPEGs in the same directory as your .aspx files. We have called ours **flower1.jpeg**, **flower2.jpeg** and **flower3.jpeg**.

The next task is to create our XML file, which describes how the **Adrotator** will function. XML files are like HTML files but they have the extension XML. The XML file for this example is listed below:

```
<Advertisements>
    <Ad>
        <ImageUrl>flower1.jpg</ImageUrl>
        <AlternateText>FlowerShop</AlternateText>
        <Impressions>35</Impressions>
        <NavigateUrl>http://www.springer.co.uk/</NavigateUrl>
    </Ad>
    <Ad>
        <ImageUrl>flower2.jpg</ImageUrl>
        <AlternateText>FlowerShop</AlternateText>
        <Impressions>35</Impressions>
```

```
              <NavigateUrl>http://www.springer.co.uk/</NavigateUrl>
      </Ad>
      <Ad>
              <ImageUrl>flower3.jpg</ImageUrl>
              <AlternateText>FlowerShop</AlternateText>
              <Impressions>30</Impressions>
              <NavigateUrl>http://www.springer.co.uk/</NavigateUrl>
      </Ad>
</Advertisements>
```

The above file can be created in the same way as your ASP.NET files and should be saved as **flower.xml** in your web server directory. Table 9.2 lists the different elements that form this file.

Table 9.2 XML AdRotator files

Element	Description
<Advertisement> </Advertisement>	There should only be one <Advertisement> element in your XML file and its tags should surround all of the other tags in the file
<Ad> </Ad>	The <Ad> element surrounds the elements that describe each advert to be displayed. You can have any number of <Ad> elements in your XML file
<ImageUrl> </ImageUrl>	Specifies the name of the image to display as the advert
<AlternateText> </AlternateText>	Specifies alternative text to be displayed if the browser viewing the page does not support graphics
<Impressions> </Impressions>	Specifies a percentage number indicating how often this particular advert should be displayed as opposed to the others
<NavigateUrl> </NavigateUrl>	Contains the URL of a web site which will be displayed if the user clicks on the advert

Our **flower.xml** file consists of three adverts, one for each of the images we created. The **AlternativeText** and **NavigateUrl** properties are the same in each of the three adverts.

When you load the **chapt9-4.aspx** file into the browser one of the adverts should be displayed. Each time you reload the page a different advert will appear randomly depending on the value contained within the Impression element.

Figure 9.5 illustrates an example of the output produced from our simple Adrotator example.

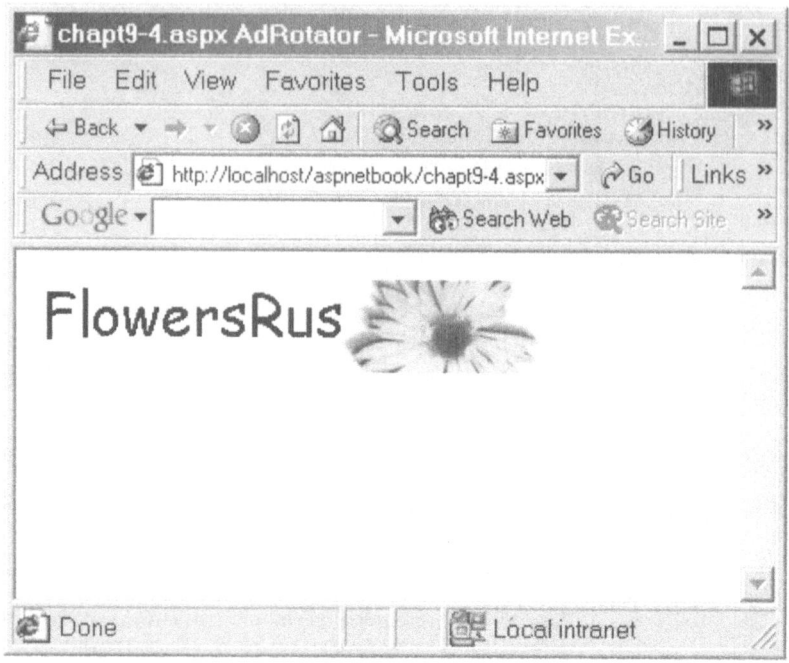

Figure 9.5 Adrotator

Summary

This chapter has introduced the **Calendar** and **Adrotator** controls and illustrated how they can be used to provide a richer user interface. In the next chapter we shall introduce the topic of form validation.

Chapter 10

Form Validation Controls

Introduction

This chapter examines the topic of validation. When interacting with users it is essential to validate that the information that a user enters is correct. For example you ask the user to enter their date of birth and they type 39/3/1969 instead of 29/3/1969. Sometimes such errors are made accidentally, other times it is deliberate. Whatever the reason it is prudent programming to validate your user input to ensure as much as possible that what you get is what you are expecting.

The Traditional Way

The traditional way of validating form input was for the developer to write code which checked each and every aspect of the form to ensure as much as possible that the data entered was correct and accurate. An example script illustrating this is shown below:

```
<%@Page Explicit="True" Language="VB" Strict="True" Debug="True" %>
<html>
    <head>
    <title>chapt10-1.aspx Traditional Form Validation</title>
    </head>

    <script runat="server">
        Sub checkForm(Sender As Object, E As EventArgs)
            Dim intErrors As Integer = 0
            firstnameLabel.Text = ""
            surnameLabel.Text = ""
            ageLabel.Text = ""
            emailLabel.Text = ""
            remailLabel.Text = ""

            If firstname.Text = "" Then
                firstnameLabel.Text = "Please enter a firstname"
```

```
                intErrors+=1
            End If
            If surname.Text = "" Then
                surnameLabel.Text = "Please enter a surname"
                intErrors+=1
            End If
            If CInt(age.Text) < 16 Or CInt(age.Text) > 70 Then
                ageLabel.Text = "Please enter an age between 16 and 70"
                intErrors+=1
            End If
            If email.Text = "" Then
                emailLabel.Text = "Please enter an email"
                intErrors+=1
            End If
            If email.Text <> remail.Text Then
                remailLabel.Text = "Email addresses do not match!"
                intErrors+=1
            End If
            If intErrors = 0 Then
                formLabel.Text = "Everything is okay"
            End If
        End Sub
    </script>

    <body>
    <h2>User Details:</h2>
    Please complete the following form:<br>
    <form runat="server">
    <table>
    <tr><td>Firstname:</td><td><asp:textbox id="firstname"
runat="server"/></td>
    <td><asp:label id="firstnameLabel" runat="server"/></td></tr>

    <tr><td>Surname:</td><td><asp:textbox id="surname" runat="server"/></td>
    <td><asp:label id="surnameLabel" runat="server"/></td></tr>

    <tr><td>Age:</td><td><asp:textbox id="age" runat="server"/></td>
    <td><asp:label id="ageLabel" runat="server"/></td></tr>

    <tr><td>Email:</td><td><asp:textbox id="email" runat="server"/></td>
    <td><asp:label id="emailLabel" runat="server"/></td></tr>
```

```
        <tr><td>ReType Email:</td><td><asp:textbox id="remail"
runat="server"/></td>
        <td><asp:label id="remailLabel" runat="server"/></td></tr>
        </table>
        <asp:button text="Submit Details" onclick="checkForm" runat="server"/>
        <br><asp:label id="formLabel" runat="server"/>
        </form>
        </body>
</html>
```

The output from this script is shown in Figure 10.1.

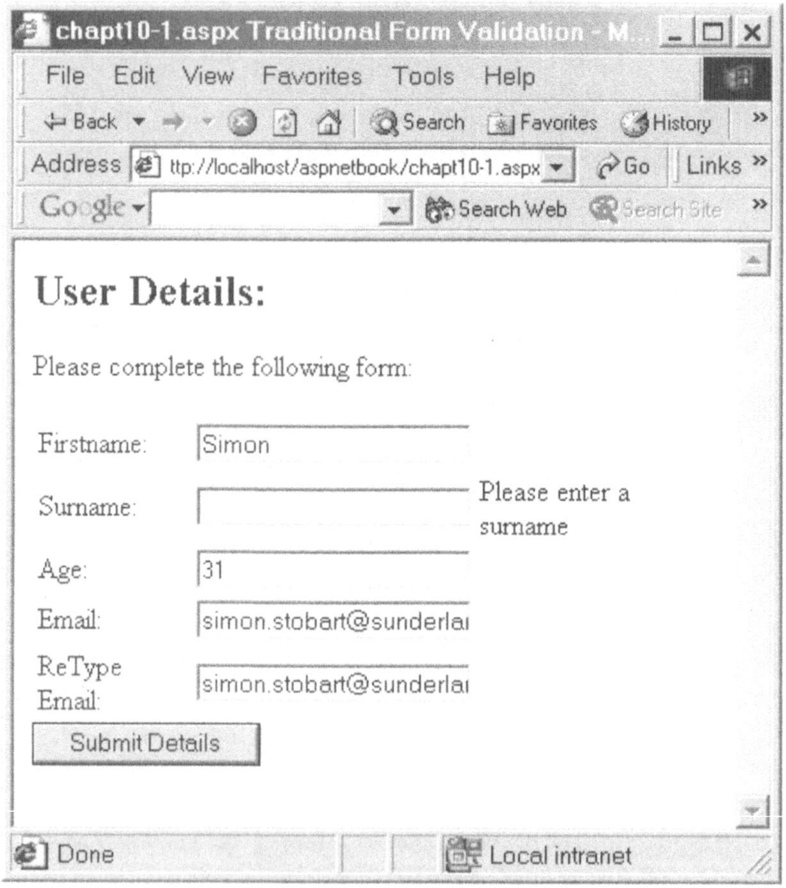

Figure 10.1 Traditional validation

The previous script contains a simple form which is submitted to subroutine **checkForm** when the form button is clicked. Subroutine **checkForm** checks the data in three different ways. Firstly to see if it is present, secondly to see if the age is within a range and thirdly to see if the two email addresses are the same.

New Validation Controls

If you have done any dynamic web programming before, the previous example should be familiar to you, certainly in terms of what it is attempting to do. When ASP.NET was developed the concept of form validation was considered important and validation controls have been built into the language to help you reduce the complexity of your applications. These validation controls are listed in Table 10.1.

Table 10.1 Validation controls

Control	Description
RequiredFieldValidator	Ensures that a value is entered or selected
CompareValidator	Compares a control value with another value or control
RangeValidator	Checks that the value is within a valid range

RequiredFieldValidator

The **RequiredFieldValidator** checks to see if a form field has been left blank. Its syntax is:

```
<asp:requiredFieldValidator id="name" controltovalidate="name" runat="server">
Error text</asp:requiredFieldValidator>
```

The tag surrounds the error message you wish to appear if the validation is false. The **controltovalidate** attribute is used to indicate which control on the form is being validated. Consider the following script, which illustrates an example of this control:

```
<%@Page Explicit="True" Language="VB" Strict="True" Debug="True" %>
<html>
     <head>
     <title>chapt10-2.aspx requiredfieldvalidator Form Validation</title>
     </head>

     <script runat="server">
          Sub checkForm(Sender As Object, E As EventArgs)
               formLabel.Text = "Everything is okay"
          End Sub
     </script>

     <body>
     <h2>User Details:</h2>
     Please complete the following form:<br>
     <form runat="server">
     <table>
     <tr><td>Firstname:</td><td><asp:textbox id="firstname"
runat="server"/></td>
     <td><asp:requiredFieldvalidator id="firstnameValid"
controltovalidate="firstname" runat="server">
     Please enter a firstname.</asp:requiredFieldvalidator></td></tr>

     <tr><td>Surname:</td><td><asp:textbox id="surname" runat="server"/></td>
     <td><asp:requiredFieldvalidator id="surnameValid"
controltovalidate="surname" runat="server">
     Please enter a surname.</asp:requiredFieldvalidator></td></tr>

     </table>
     <asp:button text="Submit Details" onclick="checkForm" runat="server"/>
     <br><asp:label id="formLabel" runat="server"/>
     </form>
     </body>
</html>
```

The above script implements a form which includes two fields, **Surname** and **Firstname**. Data must be entered into both. Note that the **checkForm** function is only invoked when all the validation controls have both been met. Figure 10.2 illustrates the output from the above script.

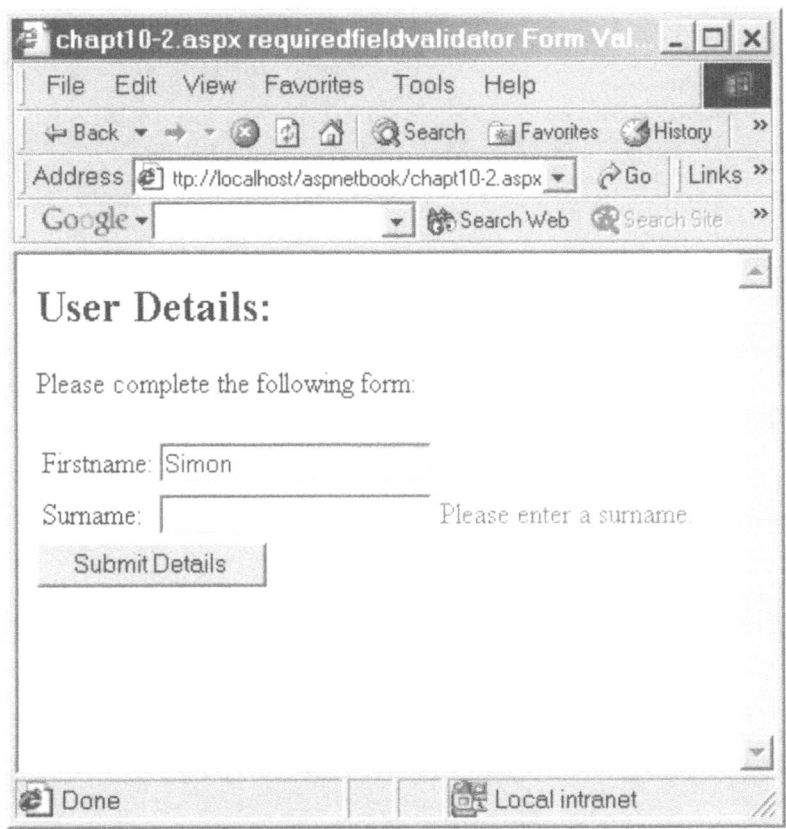

Figure 10.2 *RequiredFieldValidator*

You can use the **RequiredFieldValidator** with a list box:

```
<%@Page Explicit="True" Language="VB" Strict="True" Debug="True" %>
<html>
    <head>
    <title>chapt10-3.aspx requiredfieldvalidator with a listbox</title>
    </head>

    <script runat="server">
        Sub checkForm(Sender As Object, E As EventArgs)
            formLabel.Text = "Everything is okay"
        End Sub
```

```
</script>

<body>
<h2>User Details:</h2>
Please complete the following form:<br>
<form runat="server">
<table>
<tr><td>Sex:</td><td><asp:listbox id="sex" runat="server">
      <asp:listitem>Male</asp:listitem>
      <asp:listitem>Female</asp:listitem>
</asp:listbox></td>
<td><asp:requiredFieldvalidator id="sexValid" controltovalidate="sex"
runat="server">
Please choose a sex.</asp:requiredFieldvalidator></td></tr>

</table>
<asp:button text="Submit Details" onclick="checkForm" runat="server"/>
<br><asp:label id="formLabel" runat="server"/>
</form>
</body>
</html>
```

You can also use the **RequiredFieldValidator** with a dropdown list:

```
<%@Page Explicit="True" Language="VB" Strict="True" Debug="True" %>
<html>
    <head>
    <title>chapt10-4.aspx requiredfieldvalidator with droplist list</title>
    </head>

    <script runat="server">
        Sub checkForm(Sender As Object, E As EventArgs)
            formLabel.Text = "Everything is okay"
        End Sub
    </script>

    <body>
    <h2>User Details:</h2>
    Please complete the following form:<br>
    <form runat="server">
    <table>
    <tr><td>Sex:</td><td><asp:dropdownlist id="sex" runat="server">
```

```
        <asp:listitem>Choose Sex</asp:listitem>
        <asp:listitem>Male</asp:listitem>
        <asp:listitem>Female</asp:listitem>
    </asp:dropdownlist></td>
    <td><asp:requiredFieldvalidator id="sexValid" initialvalue="Choose Sex"
controltovalidate="sex" runat="server">
    Please choose a sex.</asp:requiredFieldvalidator></td></tr>

    </table>
    <asp:button text="Submit Details" onclick="checkForm" runat="server"/>
    <br><asp:label id="formLabel" runat="server"/>
    </form>
    </body>
</html>
```

The output from this script is shown in Figure 10.3.

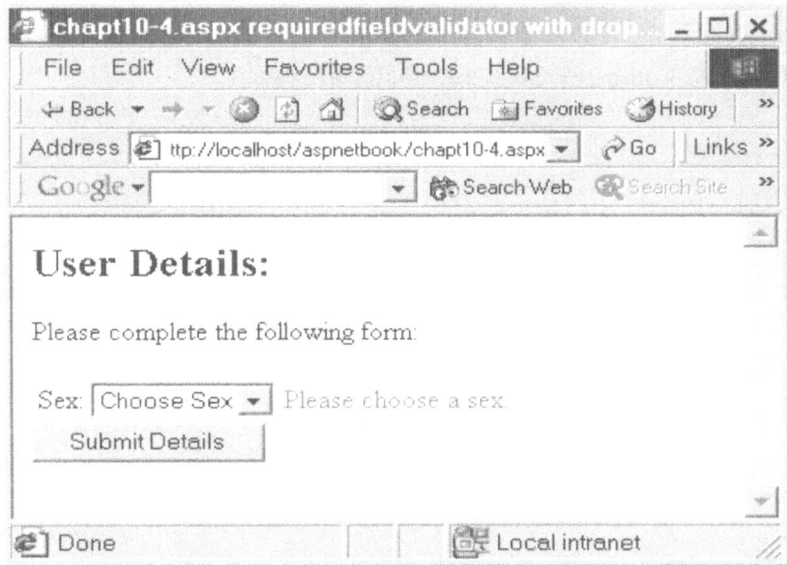

Figure 10.3 *dropdown list RequiredFieldValidator*

Notice that in the dropdown list example there is an additional attribute of the **RequiredFieldValidator**:

initialvalue="Choose Sex"

This attribute allows you to indicate an item on the list, which is initially set, but does not constitute a valid selection.

CompareValidator

The **CompareValidator** enables you to compare the value in a control to a value or another control. The syntax of the control is:

```
<asp:comparevalidator id="name" controltovalidate="name"
valuetocompare="value" operator="operator" type="type" runat="server">
```

The **CompareValidator** control has a number of attributes which can take different values. Table 10.2 lists the attributes and properties that are valid.

Table 10.2 CompareValidator attributes and values

Attribute	Values	Description
Id	Various	The id identifying this control
Controltovalidate	Various	Control that is being validated
Valuetocompare	Various	A value to compare the control against
Controltocompare	Various	The name of another control to allow the comparison of two controls
Operator	Equal NotEqual GreaterThan LessThan GreaterThanEqual LessThanEqual	How to compare the value with the control. This control is optional, it defaults to "Equal"
Type	Integer String Date Single, Etc.	The type of data being compared

The following script illustrates an example of using this control:

```
<%@Page Explicit="True" Language="VB" Strict="True" Debug="True" %>
<html>
    <head>
```

```
<title>chapt10-5.aspx compareValidator control</title>
</head>

<script runat="server">
        Sub checkForm(Sender As Object, E As EventArgs)
                formLabel.Text = "Everything is okay"
        End Sub
</script>

<body>
<h2>User Details:</h2>
Please complete the following form:<br>
<form runat="server">
<table>
<tr><td>Age:</td><td><asp:textbox id="age" runat="server"/></td>

<td><asp:comparevalidator id="ageValid" controltovalidate="age"
        valuetocompare="15" operator="GreaterThan" type="Integer"
runat="server">
    Must be greater than 15.</asp:comparevalidator></td></tr>

</table>
<asp:button text="Submit Details" onclick="checkForm" runat="server"/>
<br><asp:label id="formLabel" runat="server"/>
</form>
</body>
</html>
```

The above script illustrates the **CompareValidator** control to determine if an age entered on a form is greater than 15:

```
<asp:comparevalidator id="ageValid" controltovalidate="age" valuetocompare="15"
operator="GreaterThan" type="Integer" runat="server">
Must be greater than 15.</asp:comparevalidator></td></tr>
```

The output from the above script is illustrated in Figure 10.4. Unfortunately, while this is useful, the requirement of the developer in this instance is that the age falls between 16 and 70. The **CompareValidator** control does not allow us to accomplish this. What we need is to be able to determine if a value is within a range.

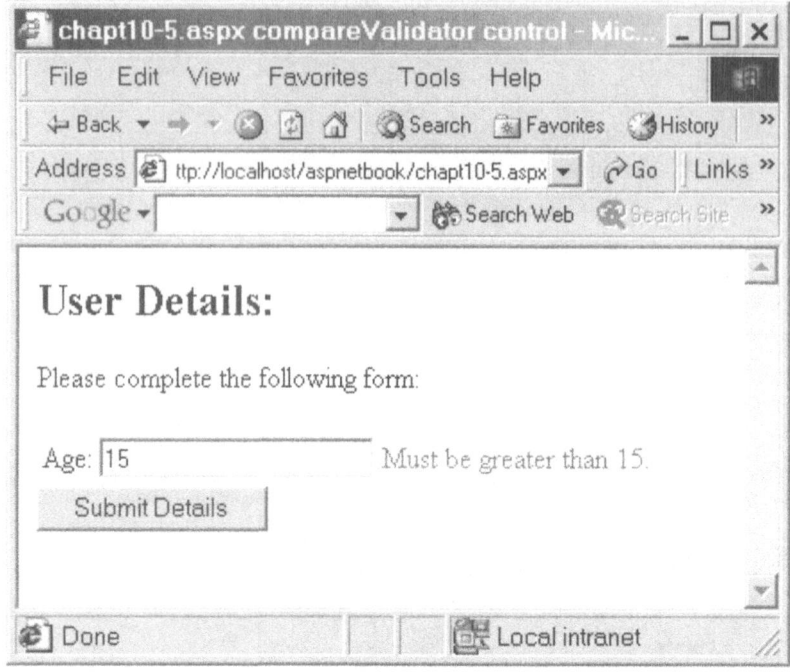

Figure 10.4 CompareValidator

RangeValidator

The RangeValidator control allows us to validate a range of numbers. Its syntax is:

```
><asp:rangevalidator id="name" controltovalidate="name" minimumvalue="value" maximumvalue="value" type="type" runat="server">
```

The RangeValidator control contains a number of different attributes. Table 10.3 lists these attributes and properties that can be used with this control.

Table 10.3 CompareValidator attributes and values

Attribute	Values	Description
Id	Various	The id identifying this control
ControltoValidate	Various	Control that is being validated
Minimumvalue	Various	Minimum value of range
Maximumvalue	Various	Maximum value of range
Type	Integer String Date Single, Etc.	The type of data being compared

The following script illustrates an example of using this control:

```
<%@Page Explicit="True" Language="VB" Strict="True" Debug="True" %>
<html>
    <head>
    <title>chapt10-6.aspx rangeValidator control</title>
    </head>

    <script runat="server">
        Sub checkForm(Sender As Object, E As EventArgs)
            formLabel.Text = "Everything is okay"
        End Sub
    </script>

    <body>
    <h2>User Details:</h2>
    Please complete the following form:<br>
    <form runat="server">
    <table>
    <tr><td>Age:</td><td><asp:textbox id="age" runat="server"/></td>

    <td><asp:rangevalidator id="ageValid" controltovalidate="age"
            minimumvalue="16" maximumvalue="70" type="Integer" runat="server">
    Must be between 16 and 70.</asp:rangevalidator></td></tr>
    </table>
    <asp:button text="Submit Details" onclick="checkForm" runat="server"/>
    <br><asp:label id="formLabel" runat="server"/>
    </form>
    </body>
</html>
```

The above script illustrates the **RangeValidator** control to determine if an age entered on a form is between 16 and 70. The output from the above script is illustrated in Figure 10.5.

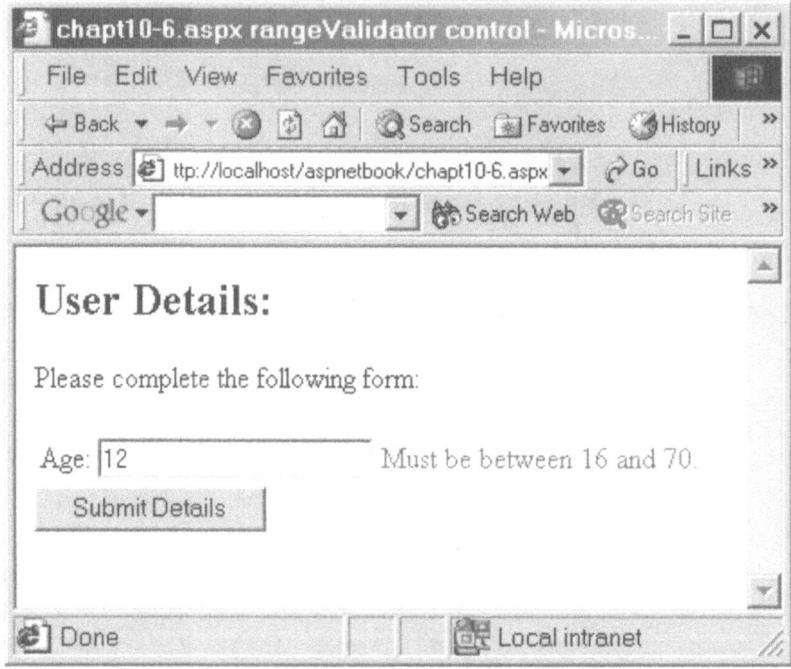

Figure 10.5 *RangeValidator*

Summary

This chapter has described some of the facilities that have been incorporated within ASP.NET to aid form validation. In the next chapter we shall examine file handling and cookies.

Chapter
11

File Handling and Cookies

Introduction

This chapter introduces file handling and cookies. In physical terms a file is a sequential collection of characters, which can be manipulated. In logical terms a file might be viewed as a collection of data records, or a computer program. Many computer systems use files for storing information for later access. A cookie is a special text file, which is created and stored by your web browser. ASP.NET has facilities to make use of and manipulate files and cookies.

Creating and Closing a File

To begin using files we must access the objects that allow us to manipulate them. This is done through the Import command:

```
<%@Import Namespace="System.IO" %>
```

The Import command loads the System.IO objects, which provide file-handling capabilities. This line is inserted near the top of your web page. The following script illustrates creating and closing a file:

```
<%@Page Explicit="True" Language="VB" Strict="True" Debug="True" %>
<%@Import Namespace="System.IO" %>
<html>
    <head>
    <title>chapt11-1.aspx Creating a File</title>
    </head>

    <script runat="server">
        Sub createFile
            Dim fileFile As textWriter
            fileFile = File.CreateText("c:\temp\myfile.txt")
            fileFile.Close
        End Sub
```

```
    </script>

    <body>
    <%createFile%>
    </body>
</html>
```

Notice the inclusion of the **Import** command at the top of the page. Also, notice that the script contains a single subroutine. This contains the code to create and close the file:

```
Sub createFile
    Dim fileFile As textWriter
    fileFile = File.CreateText("c:\temp\myfile.txt")
    fileFile.Close
End Sub
```

The first line creates an object of type **textWriter**. Essentially the **textWriter** type is a file, which can be written to. The next line invokes the **File** object **CreateText** method passing to it the name and location of a file to create. Finally, the **fileFile** object close method is invoked which closes the file and prevents any further activity with the file.

Running this script produces a blank web page. So how do we know if this has worked? Well, if you use the Windows explorer tool you should find a file called **myfile.txt** in the temporary directory of your computer.

Writing to a new file

It is all very well being able to create files and then close them, but this is not much good if you cannot write data to the file in order to store some information. The **textWriter** object has two methods, which you can use to write information to a file:

```
fileFile.Write("text")
fileFile.WriteLine("text")
```

The **Write** method allows you to write data to a file. The **WriteLine** method allows you to write some data to the file, which is then followed by a newline character. The following script provides an example of using these:

```
<%@Page Explicit="True" Language="VB" Strict="True" Debug="True" %>
<%@Import Namespace="System.IO" %>
<html>
    <head>
    <title>chapt11-2.aspx Writing to a File</title>
    </head>

    <script runat="server">
        Sub createFile
            Dim fileFile As textWriter
            fileFile = File.CreateText("c:\temp\myfile.txt")
            fileFile.Write("Hello, I am all on one")
            fileFile.Write("long line. ")
            fileFile.WriteLine("Hello, ")
            fileFile.WriteLine("I on the other hand am")
            fileFile.WriteLine("on multiple lines.")
            fileFile.Close
        End Sub
    </script>

    <body>
    <%createFile%>
    </body>
</html>
```

Again the output from this script is also blank. However if you locate the **myfile.txt** file and load this in your chosen text-editor you should find something similar to that displayed in Figure 11.1.

If you examine the contents of **myfile.txt** you should notice that it contains the text which we wrote to it in the above script. Note that the text "Hello, I am all on one long line." appears on a single line, although in the above script this was actually produced using two separate **Write** methods. This is because the **Write** methods do not insert any new-line characters after their data has been written to the file.

Furthermore, the text "I on the other hand am" and "on multiple lines" occurs on two separate lines of the file. The reason for this is that this data was written using the WriteLine methods, which does insert a new-line character at the end of each method call.

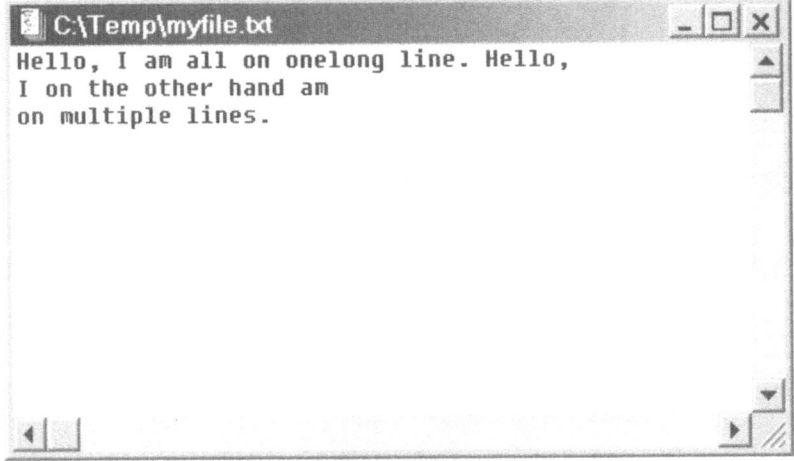

Figure 11.1 myfile.txt contents

Appending Data to a File

Once you have created a file you can continue to add data to the end of the file using the **.AppendText** method of the **File** object. The syntax is as follows:

```
fileFile = File.AppendText("filename")
```

An example of this is shown in the following script. A **While** loop has been used to add data to the end of our file:

```
<%@Page Explicit="True" Language="VB" Strict="True" Debug="True" %>
<%@Import Namespace="System.IO" %>
<html>
    <head>
```

```
      <title>chapt11-3.aspx Appending to a File</title>
      </head>
      <script runat="server">
            Sub createFile
                  Dim fileFile As textWriter
                  Dim intCount As Integer
                  fileFile = File.AppendText("c:\temp\myfile.txt")
                  For intCount = 1 To 20
                        fileFile.WriteLine("This is appended line " & intCount)
                  Next
                  fileFile.Close
            End Sub
      </script>
      <body>
      <%createFile%>
      </body>
</html>
```

The above script produces no visible output, but viewing the file it creates in your text editor should result in something similar to Figure 11.2.

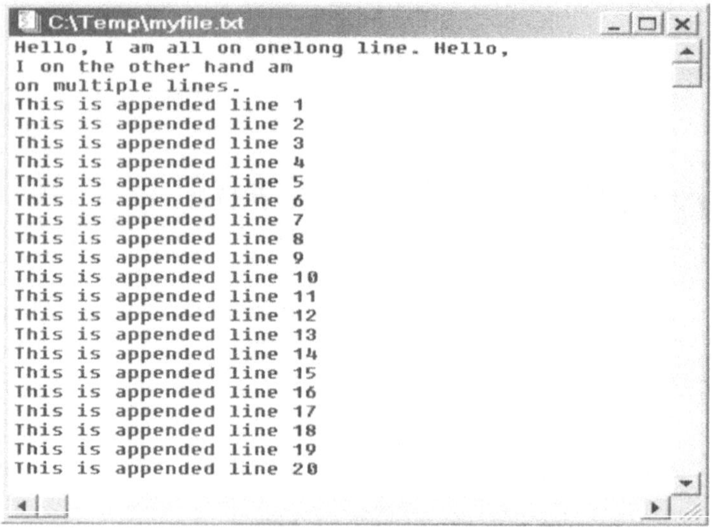

Figure 11.2 Appending data to a file

Reading a File

In addition to being able to write data to a file we also need to be able to read and access this data. The **FileOpenText** method can be used to open a file for reading, the syntax is as follows:

```
fileFile = File.OpenText("file name")
```

To read a line of text we use the **ReadLine** method, which returns a line of the file as a string:

```
strLine = fileFile.ReadLine
```

The following script illustrates the use of these methods:

```
<%@Page Explicit="True" Language="VB" Strict="True" Debug="True" %>
<%@Import Namespace="System.IO" %>
<html>
    <head>
    <title>chapt11-4.aspx Reading a File</title>
    </head>

    <script runat="server">
        Sub createFile
            Dim fileFile As textReader
            Dim strLine As String
            Dim intCount As Integer
            Response.Write("The content of the file is: <br><br>")
            If File.Exists("c:\temp\myfile.txt") Then
              fileFile = File.OpenText("c:\temp\myfile.txt")
              strLine = fileFile.ReadLine
              Do While Not (strLine Is Nothing)
                Response.Write(strLine & "<br>")
                strLine = fileFile.ReadLine
              Loop
            End If
            fileFile.Close
        End Sub
    </script>

    <body>
```

```
    <%createFile%>
    </body>
</html>
```

We also need to be able to detect when we have finished reading a file. We can check if we have reached the end of the file by determining if the line returned from the file is equal to nothing:

```
Do While Not (strLine Is Nothing)
```

Finally, it is a good idea to check if the file exists before we begin to read it. This is accomplished by using the **File.Exists** method:

```
File.Exists("c:\temp\myfile.txt")
```

The output from the above script is shown in Figure 11.3.

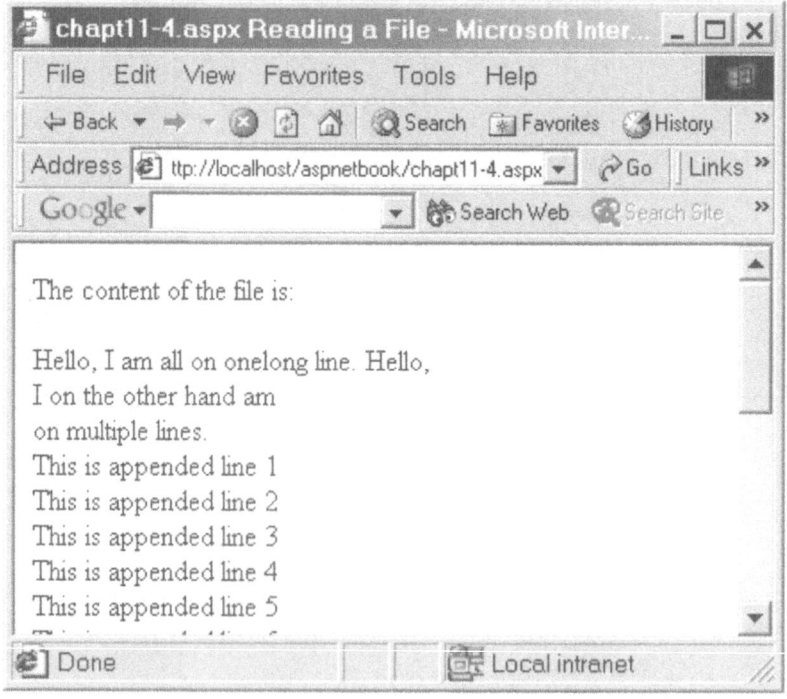

Figure 11.3 Reading a file

Cookies

Cookies are a means of storing data locally on the browser computer. They are typically used to identify users returning to a web site and to store temporary information about a web user. Essentially, a browser is capable of recording some data in a cookie, which can be assessed at a later date, sometimes months or years later.

Creating a Cookie

Creating a cookie is relatively easy. Consider the following script:

```
<%@Page Explicit="True" Language="VB" Strict="True" Debug="True" %>
<html>
    <head>
    <title>chapt11-5.aspx Setting a Cookie</title>
    </head>

    <script runat="server">
        Sub createTheCookie (Sender As Object, E As EventArgs)
            Dim myCookie As HttpCookie = New HttpCookie("YourName")
            myCookie.Values.Add("Name",NameText.Text)
            myCookie.Expires = #10/10/2003#
            Response.Cookies.Add(myCookie)
            message.text = "Cookie stored"
        End Sub
    </script>

    <body>
    <form runat="server">
    Please enter your name:<br>
    <asp:textbox id="NameText" runat="server"/>
    <asp:button text="Store as cookie" runat="server" onclick="createTheCookie"/>
    <asp:label id="message" runat="server"/>
    </form>
```

```
    </body>
</html>
```

The output from the above script is illustrated in Figure 11.4.

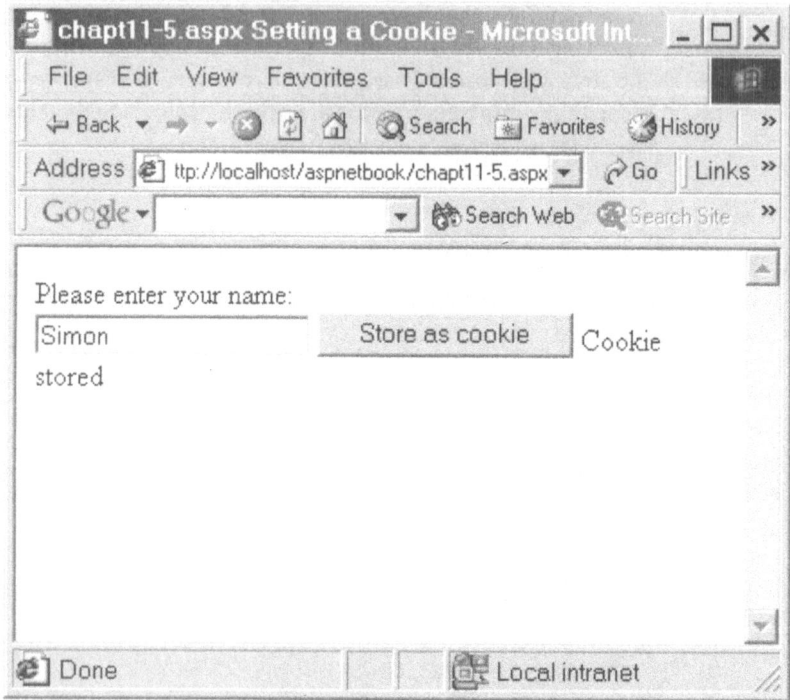

Figure 11.4 Setting a cookie

We shall now examine the previous script in some more detail. In creating a cookie you must create an object of type **HttpCookie:**

```
Dim myCookie As HttpCookie = New HttpCookie("YourName")
```

You can then assign data to the cookie. You do this using the **Values.Add** method:

```
myCookie.Values.Add("Name",NameText.Text)
```

In the above example an item called **"name"** is added to the cookie and assigned the value stored in **NameText.Text**.

Cookies can be assigned an expiry date when they are deleted from the system. This is achieved using the **Expires** method:

```
myCookie.Expires = #10/10/2003#
```

Finally the cookie is stored by using the **Response.Cookies.Add** object:

```
Response.Cookies.Add(myCookie)
```

All of the above is accomplished within the **createTheCookie** subroutine.

Viewing a Cookie

Viewing a cookie is also easy. Consider the following script:

```
<%@Page Explicit="True" Language="VB" Strict="True" Debug="True" %>
<html>
    <head>
    <title>chapt11-6.aspx Viewing a Cookie</title>
    </head>

    <script runat="server">
        Sub checkTheCookie
            Dim myCookie As HttpCookie
            myCookie = request.cookies("YourName")
            If myCookie is Nothing then
                response.Write("No cookie found")
            Else
                response.Write("Your name is : " &
request.cookies("YourName").values("Name"))
            End if
        End Sub
    </script>
    <body>
    <%checkTheCookie%>
```

```
    </body>
</html>
```

The output from the above script is illustrated in Figure 11.5.

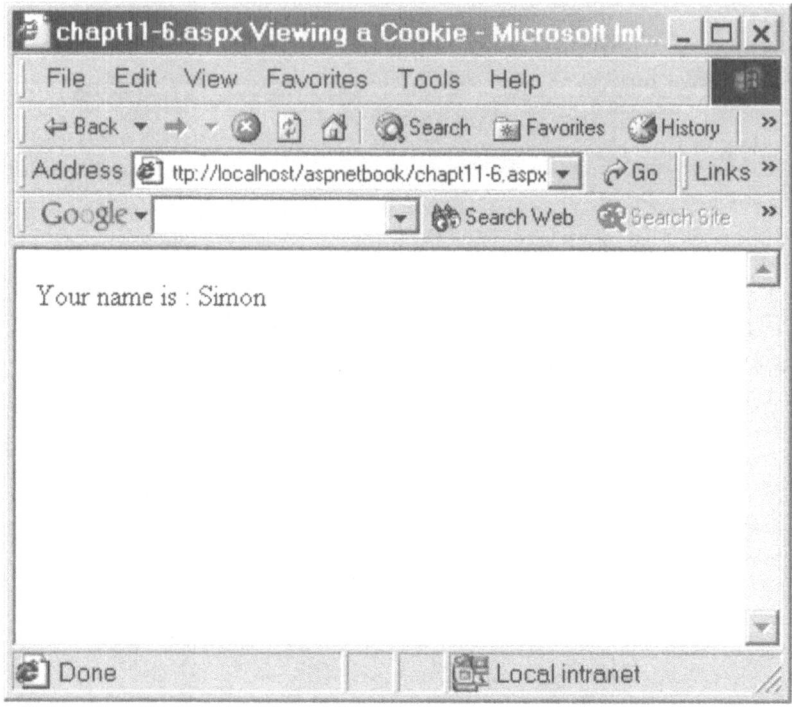

Figure 11.5 Viewing a cookie

To access a cookie you can use the **request.cookies** method:

```
myCookie = request.cookies("YourName")
```

It is a good idea to check that the returned cookie contains some information. If it does not then the cookie may have expired or was never created. To do this we can use the **"is Nothing"** expression:

```
If myCookie is Nothing then
```

```
response.Write("No cookie found")
```

To access the data stored within the cookie, we use the **request.cookies** method followed by the keyword values:

```
request.cookies("YourName").values("Name"))
```

Summary

This chapter has introduced basic file handling and cookies. You should now be able to read and write to text files and create and view cookies. In the next chapter we shall examine how the power of the database can be used with ASP.NET applications.

Chapter 12

Databases and the DataGrid

Introduction

This chapter examines how databases can be linked to web pages using the ADO.NET object library. When you can access the power of a database to retrieve and store information via a web-based system the true possibilities of what the .NET framework is capable of become clear.

This chapter illustrates the use of the **DataGrid** that enables the easy display of records returned from a database query.

What is ADO.NET?

ADO started life as ActiveX Data Objects and it was Microsoft's interface to allow easy access to many different kinds of databases. ADO has been expanded and has been incorporated within the .NET framework as a set of objects that the developer can access.

The ADO.NET library enables very complex database processes to be performed very simply without the need to worry about what is going on behind the scenes.

Importing ADO.NET

Before we can make use of the ADO.NET library of objects we need to ensure that they are available. To do this two separate **Namespaces** have to be imported at the start of your code. These are the **System.Data** and **System.data.OleDb Namespaces**. To do this the following two lines of code need to be inserted at the start of any ASP.NET program, which requires database access:

```
<%@Import Namespace="System.Data" %>
<%@Import namespace="System.Data.Oledb" %>
```

The ADO.NET Objects

There are a number of different ADO.NET objects, which are available to the developer, but Table 12.1 lists the four most common that we shall be using.

Table 12.1 ADO.NET objects

Class	Object	Description
OleDbConnection	Connection	Stores information to enable a database connection
OleDbCommand	Command	Stores the command that will be sent to the database and it also contains a Connection object in order to know what database to refer to
OleDbDataAdaptor	DataAdaptor	Wraps everything together, invoking the command to the database and retrieving the information from the database and storing it in the Dataset
Dataset	Dataset	An internal copy of part of the database

We shall explain each of these objects in turn as they can at first seem a little complex.

Connection Object

The connection object contains the details of the location and type of database you are wishing to connect to. The exact information held in the connection object thus differs depending on what type of database you are using, whether it is a Microsoft Access database or a SQL Server database for example.

To create a database connection we first declare an object of type OleDbConnection:

```
Dim myConnect As OleDbConnection;
```

The above line defines an object as being of type **OleDbConnection**. To create an instance of the object we use the new keyword:

```
myConnect = New OleDbConnection
```

The above line creates the **myConnect** object. These two separate operations can be combined into a single line:

```
Dim myConnect As OleDbConnection = New OleDbConnection
```

Having created the connection object we now need to provide it with two items of information. The first item is the name of the database provider. The database provider details the type of database you are going to access. Table 12.2 lists some common databases and the provider name.

Table 12.2 Databases and providers

Database	Provider
Microsoft Access	Microsoft.Jet.OLEDB.4.0
SQL Server	SQLOLEDB
MySQL	MySQLProv

There are many other providers for the common databases and you will need to read your database documentation to find out what they are called and where they can be obtained.

For the purposes of this chapter and introduction to databases we shall be using the Microsoft Access Provider as we shall be accessing a simple Access database.

The second item of data which must be provided is the data source. This is the name and location of the database file we wish to use.

So let's look at how we actually implement this. Firstly we need to create a string with the provider information:

```
"Provider=Microsoft.Jet.OLEDB.4.0"
```

The above string uses the keyword **Provider=** followed by the provider description, in this case the one for Microsoft

Access. Then we must include in the string the name and location of our database:

```
"Provider=Microsoft.Jet.OLEDB.4.0";Data Source=c:\cars.mdb"
```

Notice that the **Provider** string is now followed by a semicolon and then the keywords **Data Source=**. The name and location of the database is then included, which in this case is a database called **cars.mdb**.

The connection string is now complete and needs to be assigned to the appropriate property of the connection object. The name of the property to which it should be assigned is **ConnectionString** and the format for doing this is:

```
myConnect.ConnectionString = "Provider=Microsoft.Jet.OLEDB.4.0;Data
Source=c:\cars.mdb"
```

We have now finished correctly setting up the connection object. Note that we have not yet connected to the database, we have only provided the information that we need in order to do so later. The next stage is to create the command object.

Command Object

The command object is used to store the commands, which we wish to send to the database in order to obtain, delete, update or delete information. You create the command object in much the same way as we did for the connection object:

```
Dim myDbCommand As OleDbCommand = New OleDbCommand
```

The above line creates an object called **myDbCommand** of type **OleDbCommand**. The command object needs to be provided with two pieces of information. The first item is the commands which you will send to the database, and the second is the connection object which you have previously created.

The property of the command object, which stores the command text is called **CommandText** and can be assigned a command like this:

```
myDbCommand.CommandText = "Select * From Cars"
```

The above line assigns the object **myDbCommands Commandtext** property the command "Select * From Cars". This is an SQL command which requests the database to return all records from the **Cars** table. To assign the second item of information, the connection object, we use the **Connection** property:

```
myDbCommand.Connection = myConnect
```

The above command assigns the **Connection** property of the **myDbCommand** object the value of **myConnect**, which is the connection object we created earlier.

It is possible to combine the above operations into a single statement, like so:

```
Dim myDbCommand As OleDbCommand = New OleDbCommand("Select * From
Cars", myConnect)
```

The above line creates the object and assigns the command text and connection object in one operation. Either of the two ways of doing this is perfectly acceptable and you should use whichever way you feel most comfortable in using. The next stage is to create a **dataAdaptor** object that enables the connection to the database to actually happen.

DataAdaptor Object

The **dataAdaptor** object ties together the objects which we have previously created and forms a connection to the database. The first thing to do is to create an instance of a **dataAdaptor** object:

```
Dim myAdaptor As OleDbDataAdapter = New OleDbDataAdapter
```

The above line creates an object called **myAdaptor** of type OleDbDataAdaptor. The next stage is to assign the command object to the **SelectCommand** property of the **myAdaptor** object:

```
myAdaptor.SelectCommand = myDbCommand
```

All the above command does is to ensure that the **dataAdaptor** object knows which command object it is to use to form the connection. Finally, you initiate the connection to the database by invoking the **Open** method of the **Connection** object stored within the **dataAdaptor** object:

```
myAdaptor.SelectCommand.Connection.Open
```

This forms the connection between the script and the database. Unfortunately this is not the end of the story, as we also need to create an object which will store the data that is returned.

DataSet Object

All information which is returned from the database is stored in the **DataSet** object. The **DataSet** object stores information in tables and is essentially a temporary copy of part of your database. We need to begin by creating a **DataSet** object:

```
Dim CarsDataSet As DataSet = New DataSet
```

The above creates a **DataSet** object called **CarsDataSet**. To fill the dataset with data from the database we need to inform the **dataAdaptor** where to store the data. We do this by invoking the **Fill** property of the **dataAdaptor** object and pass it the **DataSet** object and a name which is the name of the table which the **DataSet** object will use to refer to this table of data:

```
myAdaptor.Fill(CarsDataSet, "Cars")
```

The above line invokes the Fill property of the **myAdaptor** object and passes it the **CarsDataSet** object and "Cars" string.

So, are we finished yet? Well while we know how to make a connection to the database and retrieve the data, which is supplied, we still do not know how to display this information.

Displaying Data

The **dataGrid** server control is used to display results obtained from a database. Essentially, the **dataGrid** is a HTML table, consisting of columns and rows which are used to output the data. In its simplest form it is very easy to use, but as we shall see it can be customized to produce some sophisticated results. In its basic form the control is used as follows:

```
<asp:datagrid id="carsTable" runat="server"/>
```

The above line illustrates the use of the **dataGrid** control. The control has one property, **id**, which is used to identify the control. In order to bind the data, which is stored in the **DataSet**, we need to specify what **DataSet** table is to be displayed in the **dataGrid**:

```
carsTable.DataSource = CarsDataSet.Tables("Cars")
```

The above line assigns the **CarsDataSetTables** called Cars to the **carsTable dataGrid** control. To actually force the data from the dataset object to the **dataGrid** control we need to invoke the server controls **DataBind** method:

```
carsTable.DataBind
```

We now have all the knowledge we need to create a script to access and display the contents of a Microsoft Access database.

Creating Our Access Database

Before you can begin to access a database from ASP.NET you will need to create one. If you are familiar with Microsoft Access and have a copy available to you then you can create your own simple database for use in these examples. If you do not then the database used in these examples is available for download with the scripts from the Essential Series web site:

www.Essential-Series.com

The file is called **cars.mdb.** If you would like to create your own copy in Microsoft Access then launch the application and set up a single database table with the field names and data types, as shown in Figure 12.1.

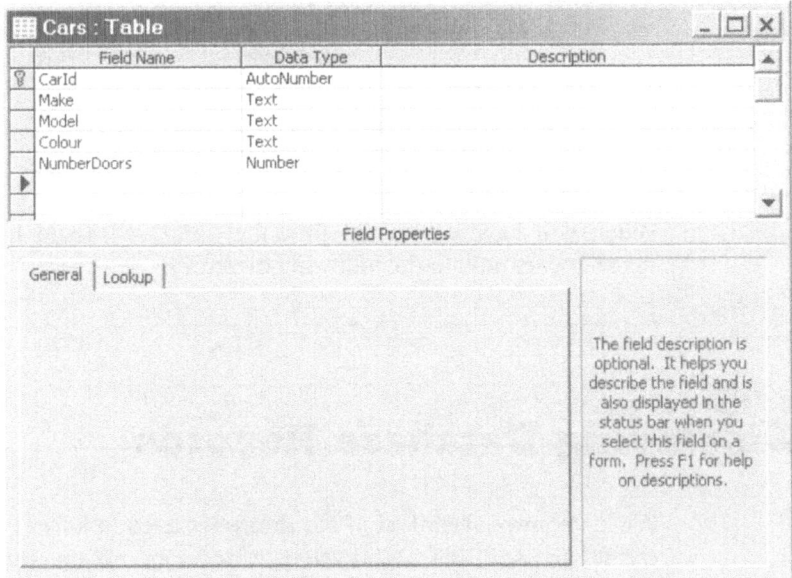

Figure 12-1 *Field names and data types*

You should also populate the database with the data shown in Figure 12.2.

Figure 12.2 Database data

When you have completed this, the database should be saved as cars.mdb in the following directory:

c:\cars.mdb

Displaying Database Records

We have now covered all of the things we need to know to create an ASP.NET application which can access and display the contents of our database. The following script illustrates an example of this:

```
<%@Page Explicit="True" Language="VB" Strict="True" Debug="True" %>
<%@Import Namespace="System.Data" %>
```

```
<%@Import namespace="System.Data.Oledb" %>
<html>
    <head>
    <title>chapt12-1.aspx Reading the Database</title>
    </head>

    <script runat="server">
        Sub Page_Load (Sender As Object, E As EventArgs)
            Dim myConnect As OleDbConnection = New OleDbConnection
            Dim myDbCommand As OleDbCommand = New OleDbCommand
            Dim myAdaptor As OleDbDataAdapter = New OleDbDataAdapter
            Dim CarsDataSet As DataSet = New DataSet

            myConnect.ConnectionString =
"Provider=Microsoft.Jet.OLEDB.4.0;Data Source=c:\cars.mdb"

            myDbCommand.CommandText = "Select * From Cars"
            myDbCommand.Connection = myConnect

            myAdaptor.SelectCommand = myDbCommand
            myAdaptor.SelectCommand.Connection.Open
            myAdaptor.Fill(CarsDataSet, "Cars")

            carsTable.DataSource = CarsDataSet.Tables("Cars")
            carsTable.DataBind
        End Sub
    </script>

    <body>
    <h1>Cars Database</h1>
    <form runat="server">
    <asp:datagrid id="carsTable" runat="server"/>
    </form>
    </body>
</html>
```

The above script combines all of the instructions we have previously examined to enable us to access some data stored in a database. The database used in the above example is the very simple **cars.mdb** database. The output generated from the above script is illustrated in Figure 12.3.

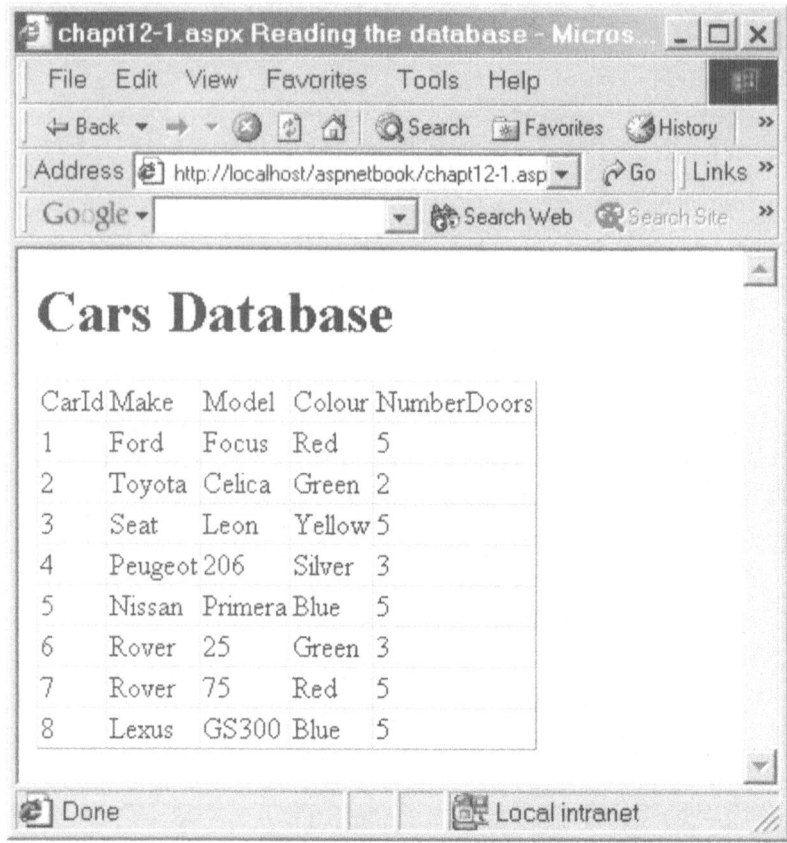

Figure 12.3 Displaying database output

Note that Figure 12.3 illustrates that all database records are neatly displayed.

DataGrid Properties

The output produced using the **DataGrid** illustrated in Figure 12.3 is very basic. However, the **DataGrid** control has a number of properties which can be used to format the output to produce a much clearer grid. Table 12-3 illustrates some of the more useful properties.

Table 12.3 DataGrid properties

Property	Description
BackColor	Background color of the grid
ForeColor	Foreground color of the grid
HorizontalAlign	Align the grid to the left, right, center
CellPadding	Specifies the cellpadding of the grid
CellSpacing	Specifies the cellspacing of the grid
Width	The width of the grid
Font-Size	The point size of the text
Font-Name	The name of the font to use

If we modify script chapt12-1.aspx, the **DataGrid** now looks like this:

```
<form runat="server">
<asp:datagrid id="carsTable" runat="server"
      BackColor="yellow"
      ForeColor="blue"
      Width="300"
      Font-Size="8pt" />
</form>
```

The output from this modified script is shown in Figure 12.4. The **DataGrid** also contains a number of styles which prove very useful in customizing how the **DataGrid** looks. The four styles supported are listed in Table 12.4.

Table 12.4 DataGrid styles

Property	Description
HeaderStyle	Specifies what the top row of the grid looks like
FooterStyle	Specifies what the bottom row of the grid looks like
ItemStyle	Specifies what each row of the grid looks like
AlternatingItemStyle	Specifies what each alternative row of the grid looks like

Each of these styles can use the properties listed in Table 12.3. The styles are inserted inside the **DataGrid** control element, for example:

```
<asp: DataGrid runat="server">
    <ItemStyle BackColor="yellow"/>
</asp:DataGrid>
```

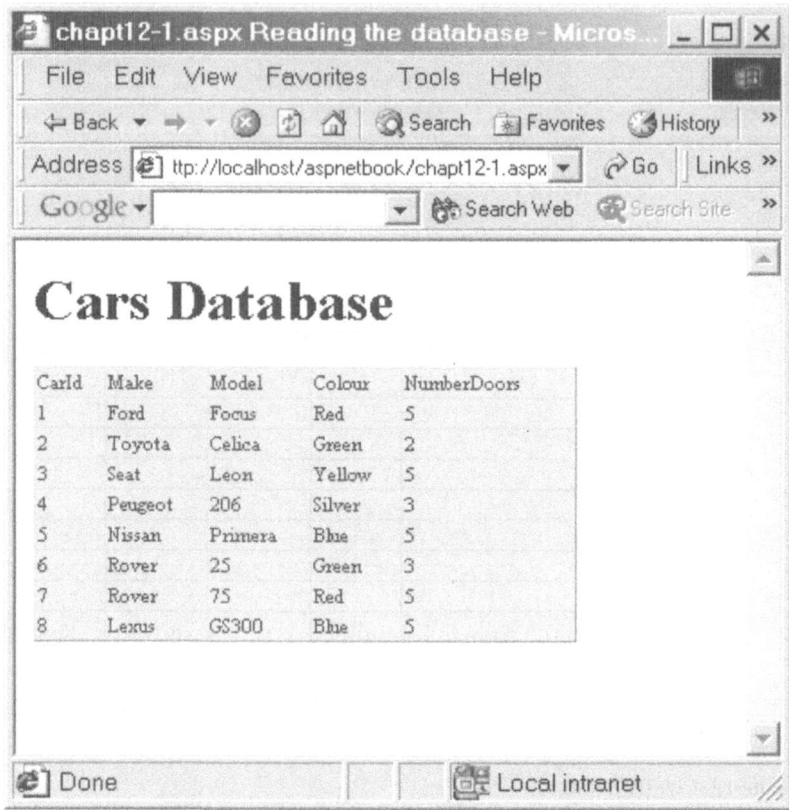

Figure 12.4 *Using DataGrid properties*

The following script illustrates an example of using **DataGrid** styles:

```
<%@Page Explicit="True" Language="VB" Strict="True" Debug="True" %>
<%@Import Namespace="System.Data" %>
<%@Import namespace="System.Data.Oledb" %>
<html>
    <head>
```

```
    <title>chapt12-2.aspx DataGrid Styles</title>
    </head>

    <script runat="server">

        Sub Page_Load (Sender As Object, E As EventArgs)
            Dim myConnect As OleDbConnection = New OleDbConnection
            Dim myDbCommand As OleDbCommand = New OleDbCommand
            Dim myAdaptor As OleDbDataAdapter = New OleDbDataAdapter
            Dim CarsDataSet As DataSet = New DataSet

            myConnect.ConnectionString =
"Provider=Microsoft.Jet.OLEDB.4.0;Data Source=c:\cars.mdb"

            myDbCommand.CommandText = "Select * From Cars"
            myDbCommand.Connection = myConnect

            myAdaptor.SelectCommand = myDbCommand
            myAdaptor.SelectCommand.Connection.Open
            myAdaptor.Fill(CarsDataSet, "Cars")

            carsTable.DataSource = CarsDataSet.Tables("Cars")
            carsTable.DataBind
        End Sub
    </script>

    <body>
    <h1>Cars Database</h1>
    <form runat="server">
    <asp:datagrid id="carsTable" runat="server">
    <HeaderStyle BackColor="blue" ForeColor="yellow" Font-Size="8pt" />
    <ItemStyle BackColor="yellow" ForeColor="blue" Font-Size="8pt" />
    <AlternatingItemStyle BackColor="white" ForeColor="blue" Font-Size="8pt" />
    </asp:datagrid>
    </form>
    </body>
</html>
```

The above script defines a **DataGrid** with three different styles, a header style, an item style and an alternating item style. The output from this script is illustrated in Figure 12.5.

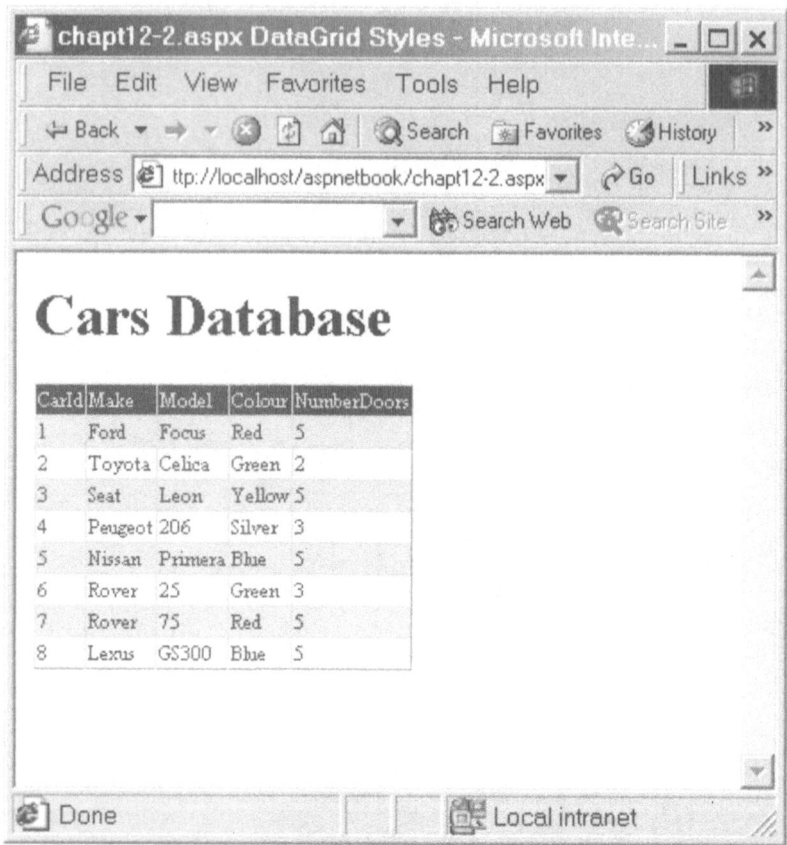

Figure 12.5 DataGrid using styles

DataGrid Columns

By default all fields from the database table are displayed in separate columns within the **DataGrid**. We can control which of these columns are displayed by turning off this property and then specifying which fields are displayed. To turn off the column fields being automatically generated we use the **DataGrid** property:

```
AutoGenerateColumns="False"
```

We then specify within the **DataGrid** element the columns to display and which fields are to be bound to each column. The syntax for doing this is:

```
<Columns>
        <asp:BoundColumn DataField="fieldname" HeaderText="Text" />
        <asp:BoundColumn DataField="fieldname" HeaderText="Text" />
        <asp:BoundColumn DataField="fieldname" HeaderText="Text" />
....
</Columns>
```

The **DataField** property specifies which database field to display in the column and the **HeaderText** property specifies the text to display in the column heading. The following script illustrates a modified **DataGrid**, which only displays certain fields from our database:

```
<%@Page Explicit="True" Language="VB" Strict="True" Debug="True" %>
<%@Import Namespace="System.Data" %>
<%@Import namespace="System.Data.Oledb" %>
<html>
        <head>
        <title>chapt12-3.aspx DataGrid Columns</title>
        </head>

        <script runat="server">

                Sub Page_Load (Sender As Object, E As EventArgs)
                        Dim myConnect As OleDbConnection = New OleDbConnection
                        Dim myDbCommand As OleDbCommand = New OleDbCommand
                        Dim myAdaptor As OleDbDataAdapter = New OleDbDataAdapter
                        Dim CarsDataSet As DataSet = New DataSet

                        myConnect.ConnectionString =
"Provider=Microsoft.Jet.OLEDB.4.0;Data Source=c:\cars.mdb"

                        myDbCommand.CommandText = "Select * From Cars"
                        myDbCommand.Connection = myConnect
```

```
            myAdaptor.SelectCommand = myDbCommand
            myAdaptor.SelectCommand.Connection.Open
            myAdaptor.Fill(CarsDataSet, "Cars")

            carsTable.DataSource = CarsDataSet.Tables("Cars")
            carsTable.DataBind
        End Sub
    </script>

<body>
<h1>Cars Database</h1>
<form runat="server">
<asp:datagrid id="carsTable" runat="server" AutoGenerateColumns="False">
<HeaderStyle BackColor="blue" ForeColor="yellow" Font-Size="8pt" />
<ItemStyle BackColor="lightgreen" ForeColor="blue" Font-Size="8pt" />
<AlternatingItemStyle BackColor="white" ForeColor="blue" Font-Size="8pt" />

<Columns>
     <asp:BoundColumn DataField="Make" HeaderText="Manufacturer" />
     <asp:BoundColumn DataField="Model" HeaderText="Model" />
     <asp:BoundColumn DataField="Colour" HeaderText="Colour" />
</Columns>
</asp:datagrid>
</form>
</body>
</html>
```

The above script introduces the **Columns** element. Three database fields are bound to three columns, **Make, Model** and **Colour**. The heading text for each of these columns is also specified. The output from this script is illustrated in Figure 12.6.

DataGrid Buttons

We may wish to display some data in a **DataGrid** and then allow the user to interact with this data. We can achieve this by specifying that one of the **DataGrid** columns is a **ButtonColumn** control:

```
<asp:ButtonColumn Text="text" HeaderText="text" />
```

The above control specifies the button text and column heading text.

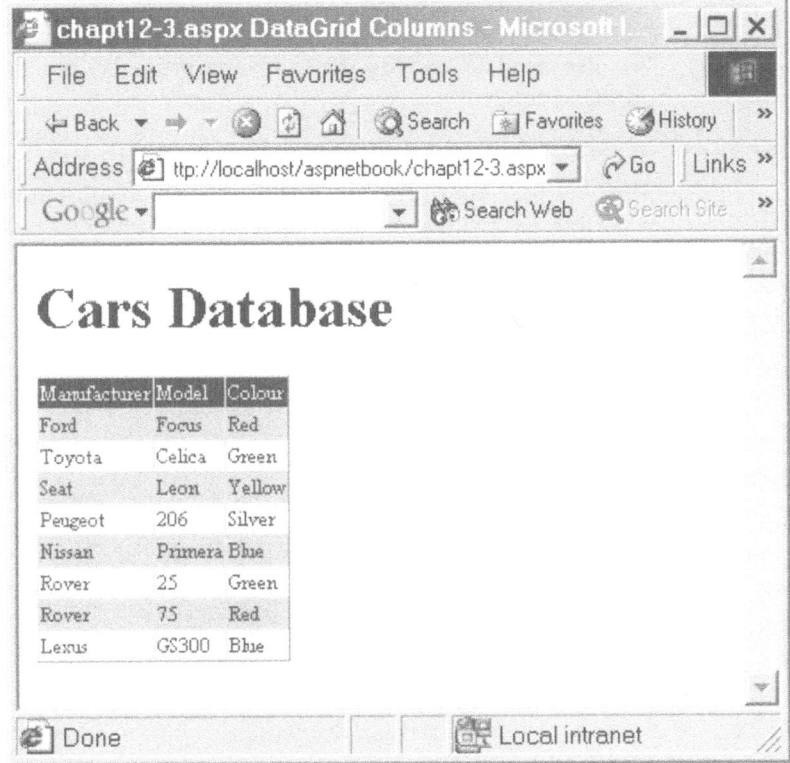

Figure 12.6 DataGrid columns

If we modify script **chapt12-3.aspx** so that the following line is inserted into the **Columns** element:

```
<asp:ButtonColumn Text="Info" HeaderText="Information" />
```

this will create a forth column with the heading Information and a text link button in each row of the table. The next step is to create an event handler, which will enable us to do something if the text button is clicked. To handle **DataGrid** event we must create a subroutine with the following definition:

```
Sub DataGridHandler (Sender As Object, E As DataGridCommandEventArgs)
...
End Sub
```

We also need to include the following property into the **DataGrid** control:

```
OnItemCommand="DataGridHandler"
```

This will pass control to the **DataGridHandler** subroutine when the user clicks on any text button. Our script now looks like this:

```
<%@Page Explicit="True" Language="VB" Strict="True" Debug="True" %>
<%@Import Namespace="System.Data" %>
<%@Import namespace="System.Data.Oledb" %>
<html>
    <head>
    <title>chapt12-4.aspx DataGrid Buttons</title>
    </head>

    <script runat="server">

        Sub Page_Load (Sender As Object, E As EventArgs)
            Dim myConnect As OleDbConnection = New OleDbConnection
            Dim myDbCommand As OleDbCommand = New OleDbCommand
            Dim myAdaptor As OleDbDataAdapter = New OleDbDataAdapter
            Dim CarsDataSet As DataSet = New DataSet

            myConnect.ConnectionString =
"Provider=Microsoft.Jet.OLEDB.4.0;Data Source=c:\cars.mdb"

            myDbCommand.CommandText = "Select * From Cars"
            myDbCommand.Connection = myConnect

            myAdaptor.SelectCommand = myDbCommand
            myAdaptor.SelectCommand.Connection.Open
            myAdaptor.Fill(CarsDataSet, "Cars")

            carsTable.DataSource = CarsDataSet.Tables("Cars")
            carsTable.DataBind
```

```
        End Sub

        Sub DataGridHandler (Sender As Object, E As
DataGridCommandEventArgs)
                Response.Write("You clicked a button")
        End Sub

    </script>

    <body>
    <h1>Cars Database</h1>
    <form runat="server">
    <asp:datagrid id="carsTable"
        runat="server"
        AutoGenerateColumns="False"
        OnItemCommand="DataGridHandler">

    <HeaderStyle BackColor="blue" ForeColor="yellow" Font-Size="8pt" />
    <ItemStyle BackColor="lightgreen" ForeColor="blue" Font-Size="8pt" />
    <AlternatingItemStyle BackColor="white" ForeColor="blue" Font-Size="8pt" />

    <Columns>
        <asp:BoundColumn DataField="Make" HeaderText="Manufacturer" />
        <asp:BoundColumn DataField="Model" HeaderText="Model" />
        <asp:BoundColumn DataField="Colour" HeaderText="Colour" />

        <asp:ButtonColumn Text="Info" HeaderText="Information" />
    </Columns>
    </asp:datagrid>
    </form>
    </body>
</html>
```

The above script includes the **ButtonColumn** control to create a text button column. The **OnItemCommand** property of the **DataGrid** control ensures that the subroutine **DataGridHandler** will be invoked when any button is clicked. The subroutine displays the text "**You clicked a button**".

Figure 12.7 illustrates the output from the above script.

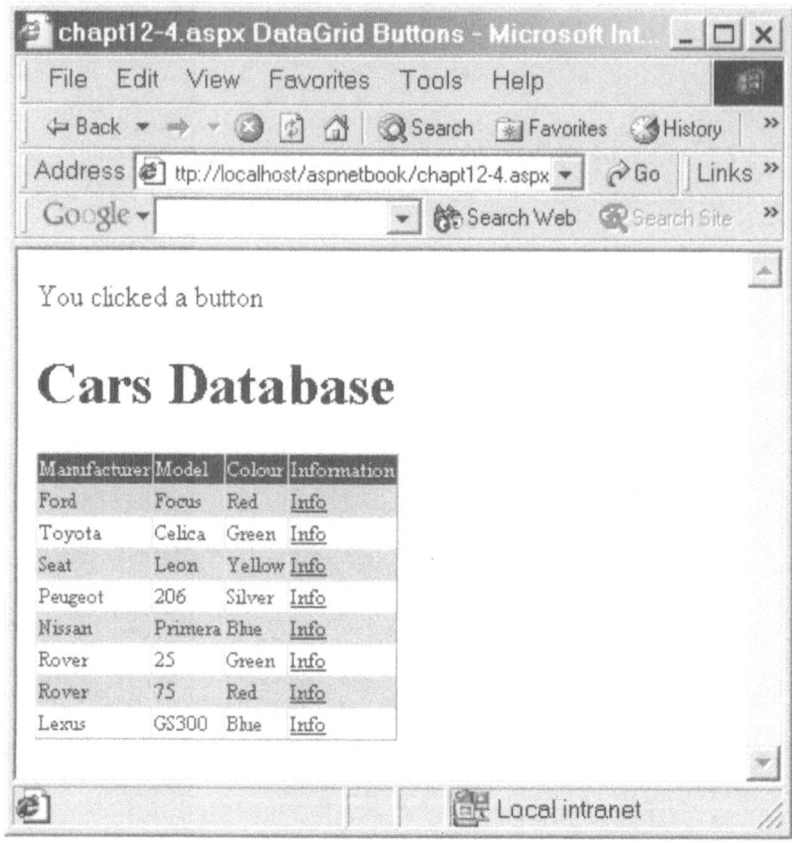

Figure 12.7 *DataGrid buttons*

The above script is not all that useful at the moment. What we really need to be able to do is to determine which of the row buttons was clicked. Why? Well, if we know which button was clicked then we can do something that is specific that particular data item.

To access the data on the row on which the text button was clicked we need to create an object of type **TableCell**:

```
Dim columnName as TableCell
```

The cell of the first column of the selected row can be copied into this object using a subscripted reference:

```
ColumnName = e.Item.Cells(0)
```

To access the contents of the cell the **e.Item.Cells.Text** property can be accessed:

```
Dim cellText As String = ColumnName.Text
```

The following script illustrates accessing the data in a row of a **DataGrid**:

```
<%@Page Explicit="True" Language="VB" Strict="True" Debug="True" %>
<%@Import Namespace="System.Data" %>
<%@Import namespace="System.Data.Oledb" %>
<html>
    <head>
    <title>chapt12-5.aspx DataGrid Cell Accessing</title>
    </head>

    <script runat="server">

        Sub Page_Load (Sender As Object, E As EventArgs)
            Dim myConnect As OleDbConnection = New OleDbConnection
            Dim myDbCommand As OleDbCommand = New OleDbCommand
            Dim myAdaptor As OleDbDataAdapter = New OleDbDataAdapter
            Dim CarsDataSet As DataSet = New DataSet

            myConnect.ConnectionString =
"Provider=Microsoft.Jet.OLEDB.4.0;Data Source=c:\cars.mdb"

            myDbCommand.CommandText = "Select * From Cars"
            myDbCommand.Connection = myConnect

            myAdaptor.SelectCommand = myDbCommand
            myAdaptor.SelectCommand.Connection.Open
            myAdaptor.Fill(CarsDataSet, "Cars")

            carsTable.DataSource = CarsDataSet.Tables("Cars")
            carsTable.DataBind
        End Sub
```

```
        Sub DataGridHandler (Sender As Object, E As
DataGridCommandEventArgs)
            Dim idColumn As TableCell = e.Item.Cells(0)
            Dim strCarId as String = idColumn.Text
            Response.Write("You clicked button # " + strCarId)
        End Sub

</script>

<body>
<h1>Cars Database</h1>
<form runat="server">
<asp:datagrid id="carsTable"
      runat="server"
      AutoGenerateColumns="False"
      OnItemCommand="DataGridHandler">

<HeaderStyle BackColor="blue" ForeColor="yellow" Font-Size="8pt" />
<ItemStyle BackColor="lightgreen" ForeColor="blue" Font-Size="8pt" />
<AlternatingItemStyle BackColor="white" ForeColor="blue" Font-Size="8pt" />

<Columns>
      <asp:BoundColumn DataField="CarId" Visible="False" />
      <asp:BoundColumn DataField="Make" HeaderText="Manufacturer" />
      <asp:BoundColumn DataField="Model" HeaderText="Model" />
      <asp:BoundColumn DataField="Colour" HeaderText="Colour" />
      <asp:ButtonColumn Text="Info" HeaderText="Information" />
</Columns>
</asp:datagrid>
</form>
</body>
</html>
```

The above script displays the number of the row on which the text button was clicked. It does this by including a bound **DataField** as a column but this is hidden from view by the Visible="false" property:

```
<asp:BoundColumn DataField="CarId" Visible="False" />
```

The **DataGridHandler** subroutine accesses this cell data and displays the number held within the field:

```
Dim idColumn As TableCell = e.Item.Cells(0)
```

The result of which is illustrated in Figure 12.8.

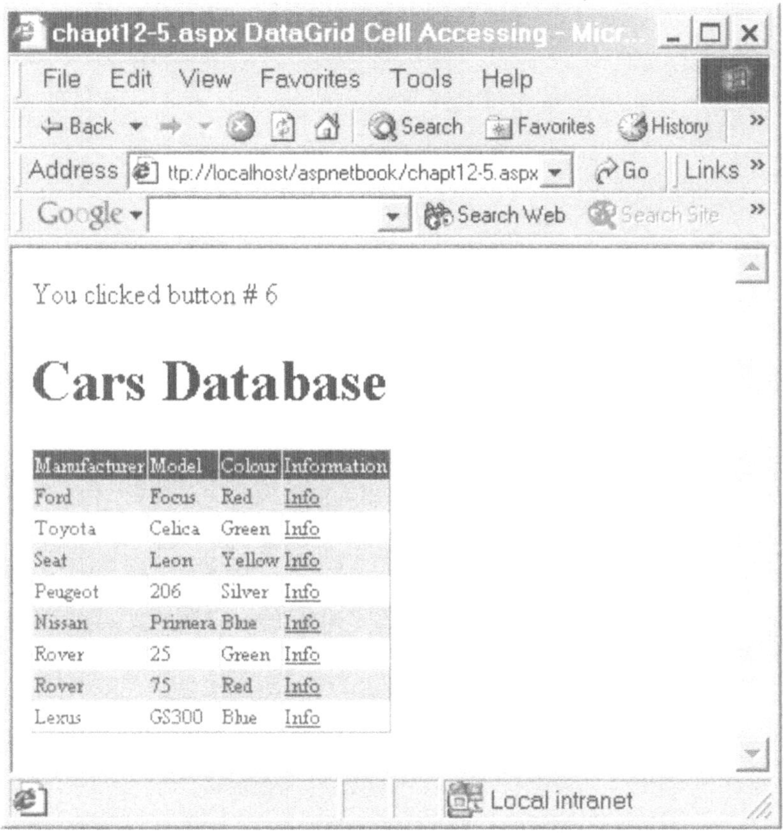

Figure 12.8 *Accessing an individual cell*

DataGrid Paging

In our examples so far using the **DataGrid**, all the database records are displayed. Of course this does not really matter with our database because we only have a handful of records. If however our database contained many records we would need to implement some form of paging to allow only a certain number of records to be displayed on each page. Consider the following script:

```
<%@Page Explicit="True" Language="VB" Strict="True" Debug="True" %>
<%@Import Namespace="System.Data" %>
<%@Import namespace="System.Data.Oledb" %>
<html>
    <head>
    <title>chapt12-6.aspx Paging Database Results</title>
    </head>

    <script runat="server">

        Sub ButtonNClick (Sender As Object, E As EventArgs)
            If (carsTable.CurrentPageIndex < (carsTable.PageCount-1)) Then
                carsTable.CurrentPageIndex += 1
            End If
            Page.DataBind
        End Sub

        Sub ButtonPClick (Sender As Object, E As EventArgs)
            If (carsTable.CurrentPageIndex > 0) Then
                carsTable.CurrentPageIndex -= 1
            End If
            Page.DataBind
        End Sub

        Sub Page_Load (Sender As Object, E As EventArgs)
            Dim myConnect As OleDbConnection = New OleDbConnection
            Dim myDbCommand As OleDbCommand = New OleDbCommand
            Dim myAdaptor As OleDbDataAdapter = New OleDbDataAdapter
            Dim CarsDataSet As DataSet = New DataSet

            myConnect.ConnectionString =
"Provider=Microsoft.Jet.OLEDB.4.0;Data Source=c:\cars.mdb"

            myDbCommand.CommandText = "Select * From Cars"
            myDbCommand.Connection = myConnect

            myAdaptor.SelectCommand = myDbCommand
```

```
                myAdaptor.SelectCommand.Connection.Open
                myAdaptor.Fill(CarsDataSet, "Cars")

                carsTable.DataSource = CarsDataSet.Tables("Cars")
                carsTable.DataBind
        End Sub
    </script>

    <body>
    <h1>Cars Database</h1>
    <form runat="server">
    <asp:datagrid id="carsTable" runat="server"
        AllowPaging="True"
        PagerStyle-Visible="False"
        Pagesize="5"
        AutoGenerateColumns="False">

    <HeaderStyle BackColor="blue" ForeColor="yellow" Font-Size="8pt" />
    <ItemStyle BackColor="lightgreen" ForeColor="blue" Font-Size="8pt" />
    <AlternatingItemStyle BackColor="white" ForeColor="blue" Font-Size="8pt" />

    <Columns>
            <asp:BoundColumn DataField="CarId" Visible="False" />
            <asp:BoundColumn DataField="Make" HeaderText="Manufacturer" />
            <asp:BoundColumn DataField="Model" HeaderText="Model" />
            <asp:BoundColumn DataField="Colour" HeaderText="Colour" />

    </Columns>
    </asp:datagrid>
    <asp:linkbutton id="Prevbutton" Text="Prev" CommandArgument="Prev"
runat="server"
        onclick="ButtonPClick"/>
    <asp:linkbutton id="Nextbutton" Text="Next" CommandArgument="Next"
runat="server"
        onclick="ButtonNClick"/>
    </form>
    </body>
</html>
```

The above script implements a paged **DataGrid**, which displays a maximum of five records per page and allows the user to move to the next and previous pages by clicking on a linkButton.

The output from the above script is illustrated in Figure 12.9.

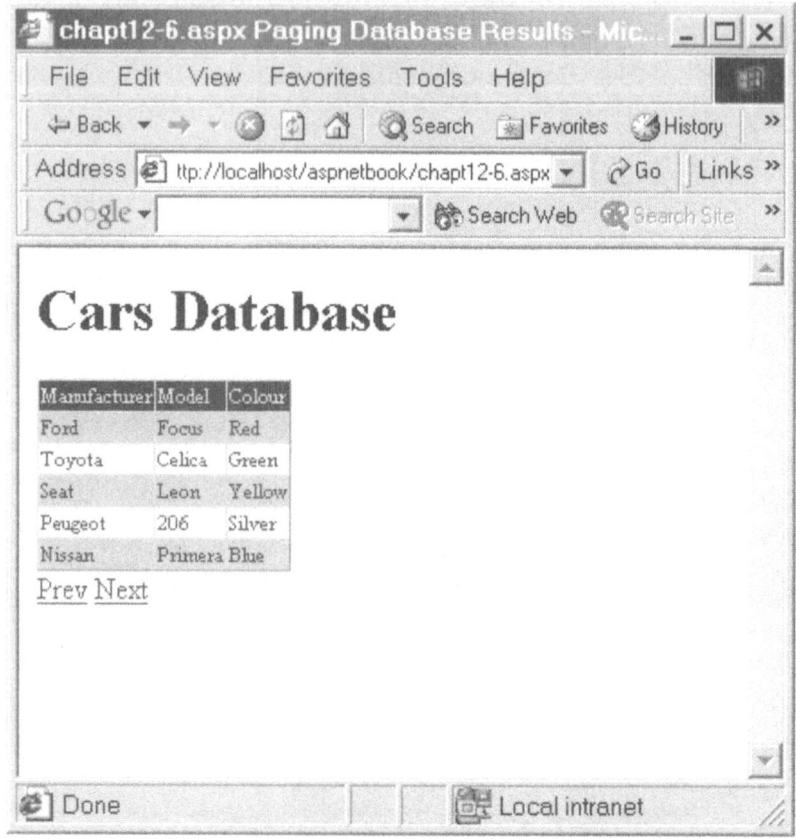

Figure 12.9 *DataGrid paging*

Let's examine how the script works. The **dataGrid** control contains some new properties:

```
<asp:datagrid id="carsTable" runat="server"
        AllowPaging="True"
        PagerStyle-Visible="False"
```

```
Pagesize="5"
```

The **AllowPaging** control allows the **DataGrid** to be paged. The **PagerStyle-Visible** control allows us to turn off the default **DataGrid** paging controls so that we can create some of our own. The **PageSize** control sets the number of records which can be displayed on a page.

The form also contains two link buttons which allow us to move between the separate pages of records:

```
<asp:linkbutton id="Prevbutton" Text="Prev" CommandArgument="Prev"
runat="server" onclick="ButtonPClick"/>
<asp:linkbutton id="Nextbutton" Text="Next" CommandArgument="Next"
runat="server" onclick="ButtonNClick"/>
```

When one of these link buttons is clicked, one of the following subroutines is invoked:

```
Sub ButtonNClick (Sender As Object, E As EventArgs)
        If (carsTable.CurrentPageIndex < (carsTable.PageCount-1)) Then
            carsTable.CurrentPageIndex += 1
        End If
        Page.DataBind
End Sub

Sub ButtonPClick (Sender As Object, E As EventArgs)
        If (carsTable.CurrentPageIndex > 0) Then
            carsTable.CurrentPageIndex -= 1
        End If
        Page.DataBind
End Sub
```

These subroutines use the **CurrentPageIndex** and the **PageCount** methods of the **DataGrid** to determine which records to display. The **Page.DataBind** method is then invoked to redisplay the fields within the **DataGrid**.

Summary

This chapter has introduced databases and how they can be accessed from within an ASP.NET script. The basic commands to create a link to a database have been described. The **DataGrid** control has been introduced and some of its many features have been examined and illustrated. In the following chapter we shall continue our examination of databases by introducing some further ways that we can interact with them.

Chapter 13

Interacting with Databases

Introduction

This chapter examines how you can manipulate the content of a database using various ADO.NET controls. Examples of script to add, update and delete records are included.

Adding Records

To add a record to a database an **OleDbConnection** to the database has to be created:

```
myConnection = New OleDbConnection("Provider=Microsoft.Jet.OLEDB.4.0;Data
Source=c:\cars.mdb")
```

Next, a connection to the database needs to be opened:

```
myConnection.Open()
```

The SQL command to add records to a database is **INSERT** and this is passed as a parameter to the **OleDbCommand** class:

```
myCommand = New OleDbCommand("INSERT INTO Cars
(Make,Model,Colour,NumberDoors) VALUES ('Ford','Ka','Red','2')",myConnection)
```

Next, the above command is executed using the **ExecuteNonQuery** method of the **Command** class:

```
myCommand.ExecuteNonQuery()
```

This method is used to execute SQL statements, which do not return any database records. Finally, the connection to the database is closed:

```
myConnection.Close()
```

The following script illustrates the use of these commands:

```
<%@Page Explicit="True" Language="VB" Strict="True" Debug="True" %>
<%@Import Namespace="System.Data" %>
<%@Import namespace="System.Data.Oledb" %>
```

```
<html>
    <head>
    <title>chapt13-1.aspx Adding Database Records</title>
    </head>

    <script runat="server">

        Sub Page_Load (Sender As Object, E As EventArgs)
            Display()
        End Sub

        Sub Display ()
            Dim strConnection As String =
"Provider=Microsoft.Jet.OLEDB.4.0;Data Source=c:\cars.mdb"
            Dim strCommand As String = "Select * From Cars"
            Dim myConnect As OleDbConnection = New OleDbConnection
            Dim myAdaptor As OleDbDataAdapter = New OleDbDataAdapter
            Dim CarsDataSet As DataSet = New DataSet
            myConnect.ConnectionString = strConnection
            myAdaptor.SelectCommand = New
OleDbCommand(strCommand,myConnect)
            myAdaptor.SelectCommand.Connection.Open

            myAdaptor.Fill(CarsDataSet, "Cars")

            carsTable.DataSource = CarsDataSet.Tables("Cars")
            carsTable.DataBind
        End Sub

        Sub DataGridAdd (Sender As Object, E As EventArgs)

            Dim strAdd As String

            strAdd = "('" & Manufacturer.Text & "','" & Model.Text & "','" &
Colour.Text & "','" & NumberDoors.Text & "')"

            Dim myConnection As OleDbConnection
            Dim myCommand As OleDbCommand

            myConnection = New
OleDbConnection("Provider=Microsoft.Jet.OLEDB.4.0;Data Source=c:\cars.mdb")
```

```
                myConnection.Open()

                myCommand = New OleDbCommand("INSERT INTO Cars
(Make,Model,Colour,NumberDoors) VALUES " & strAdd,myConnection)

                myCommand.ExecuteNonQuery()
                myConnection.Close()
                display()
        End Sub

    </script>

    <body>
    <h1>Cars Database</h1>
    <form runat="server">
    <asp:datagrid id="carsTable" runat="server"
        AutoGenerateColumns="False">

    <HeaderStyle BackColor="blue" ForeColor="yellow" Font-Size="8pt" />
    <ItemStyle BackColor="lightgreen" ForeColor="blue" Font-Size="8pt" />
    <AlternatingItemStyle BackColor="white" ForeColor="blue" Font-Size="8pt" />

    <Columns>
        <asp:BoundColumn DataField="CarId" HeaderText="CarId" />
        <asp:BoundColumn DataField="Make" HeaderText="Manufacturer" />
        <asp:BoundColumn DataField="Model" HeaderText="Model" />
        <asp:BoundColumn DataField="Colour" HeaderText="Colour" />
        <asp:BoundColumn DataField="NumberDoors"
HeaderText="NumberDoors" />
    </Columns>
    </asp:datagrid>
    Manufacturer:<br>
    <asp:textbox id="Manufacturer" runat="server"/><br>
    Model:<br>
    <asp:textbox id="Model" runat="server"/><br>
    Colour:<br>
    <asp:textbox id="Colour" runat="server"/><br>
    Number of Doors:<br>
    <asp:textbox id="NumberDoors" runat="server"/><br>
    <asp:button text="Add" runat="server" onclick="DataGridAdd"/>
    </form>
    </body>
```

```
</html>
```

The output from the above script is illustrated in Figure 13.1.

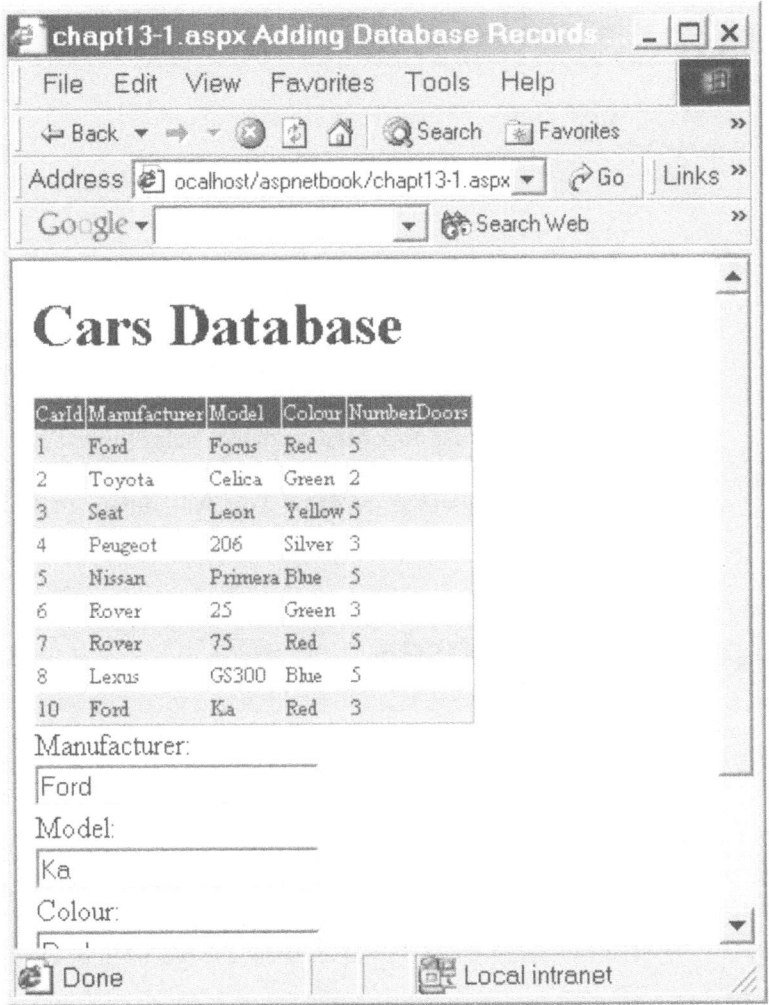

Figure 13.1 *Adding records*

The above script uses a **DataGrid** to display the contents of the database. The **DataGrid** was introduced in the previous chapter and the example employed in the above script is exactly the same.

In addition to the DataGrid the form element has a number of textbox controls:

```
<asp:textbox id="Manufacturer" runat="server"/><br>
Model:<br>
<asp:textbox id="Model" runat="server"/><br>
Colour:<br>
<asp:textbox id="Colour" runat="server"/><br>
Number of Doors:<br>
<asp:textbox id="NumberDoors" runat="server"/><br>
```

When the form button is clicked, subroutine **DataGridAdd** is invoked. This subroutine forms a connection to the database **cars.mdb** and inserts the data into the database. After the database has been updated, subroutine **Display** reads the database records and using the **DataGrid** displays the updated database records. You will notice that the recently added record is then displayed.

Updating Records

The updating of database records is very similar to that of adding records. The only difference is with the **OleDbCommand** parameter, which now employs the UPDATE command:

```
myCommand = New OleDbCommand("UPDATE Cars SET Model='Ford' WHERE
CarId='4',myConnection)
```

The following script illustrates database record updating:

```
<%@Page Explicit="True" Language="VB" Strict="True" Debug="True" %>
<%@Import Namespace="System.Data" %>
<%@Import namespace="System.Data.Oledb" %>
<html>
    <head>
    <title>chapt13-2.aspx Updating Database Records</title>
```

```
</head>

<script runat="server">

        Sub Page_Load (Sender As Object, E As EventArgs)
                Display()
        End Sub

        Sub Display ()
                Dim strConnection As String =
"Provider=Microsoft.Jet.OLEDB.4.0;Data Source=c:\cars.mdb"
                Dim strCommand As String = "Select * From Cars"
                Dim myConnect As OleDbConnection = New OleDbConnection
                Dim myAdaptor As OleDbDataAdapter = New OleDbDataAdapter
                Dim CarsDataSet As DataSet = New DataSet
                myConnect.ConnectionString = strConnection
                myAdaptor.SelectCommand = New
OleDbCommand(strCommand,myConnect)
                myAdaptor.SelectCommand.Connection.Open

                myAdaptor.Fill(CarsDataSet, "Cars")

                carsTable.DataSource = CarsDataSet.Tables("Cars")
                carsTable.DataBind
        End Sub

        Sub DataGridUpdate (Sender As Object, E As EventArgs)

                Dim strUpdate As String

                strUpdate = "Make='" & Manufacturer.Text & "',Model='" &
Model.Text & "',Colour='" & Colour.Text & "',NumberDoors='" & NumberDoors.Text & "'"

                Dim myConnection As OleDbConnection
                Dim myCommand As OleDbCommand


                myConnection = New
OleDbConnection("Provider=Microsoft.Jet.OLEDB.4.0;Data Source=c:\cars.mdb")
                myConnection.Open()
```

```
            myCommand = New OleDbCommand("UPDATE Cars SET " &
strUpdate & " WHERE CarId= " & CarId.Text,myConnection)

            myCommand.ExecuteNonQuery()
            myConnection.Close()
            display()
        End Sub

    </script>

    <body>
    <h1>Cars Database</h1>
    <form runat="server">
    <asp:datagrid id="carsTable" runat="server"
        AutoGenerateColumns="False">

    <HeaderStyle BackColor="blue" ForeColor="yellow" Font-Size="8pt" />
    <ItemStyle BackColor="lightgreen" ForeColor="blue" Font-Size="8pt" />
    <AlternatingItemStyle BackColor="white" ForeColor="blue" Font-Size="8pt" />

    <Columns>
        <asp:BoundColumn DataField="CarId" HeaderText="CarId" />
        <asp:BoundColumn DataField="Make" HeaderText="Manufacturer" />
        <asp:BoundColumn DataField="Model" HeaderText="Model" />
        <asp:BoundColumn DataField="Colour" HeaderText="Colour" />

        <asp:BoundColumn DataField="NumberDoors"
HeaderText="NumberDoors" />
    </Columns>
    </asp:datagrid>

    CarId:<br>
    <asp:textbox id="CarId" runat="server"/><br>
    Manufacturer:<br>
    <asp:textbox id="Manufacturer" runat="server"/><br>
    Model:<br>
    <asp:textbox id="Model" runat="server"/><br>
    Colour:<br>
    <asp:textbox id="Colour" runat="server"/><br>
    Number of Doors:<br>
    <asp:textbox id="NumberDoors" runat="server"/><br>
    <asp:button text="Add" runat="server" onclick="DataGridUpdate"/>
```

```
    </form>
    </body>
</html>
```

The above script uses a form to enable the user to enter data to allow a record to be updated. Notice that an additional form **textbox** is used to allow the user to enter the **CarId**:

```
CarId:<br>
<asp:textbox id="CarId" runat="server"/><br>
```

The **CarId textbox** is used by the user to specify which database record will be updated. **CarId** is the primary database key and is unique. By providing a valid **CarId** the script is able to determine which database record the user wishes to update.

This script does not contain any error checking. If the user wishes to only update one field of a database record they still will need to supply the original values of the fields via form or this data will be lost. An obvious amendment to this script would be to allow the user to enter into the form only the data that the user wished to change. Any textbox which was left empty would indicate that the original data in this database field should be left unchanged.

Note also that the form data is not cleared when the user clicks the submit button. The **Display** subroutine is the same as that in the previous example. The **DataGridAdd** subroutine has been renamed **DataGridUpdate**, but apart from the use of the UPDATE command they are the same.

The output from this script is illustrated in Figure 13.2.

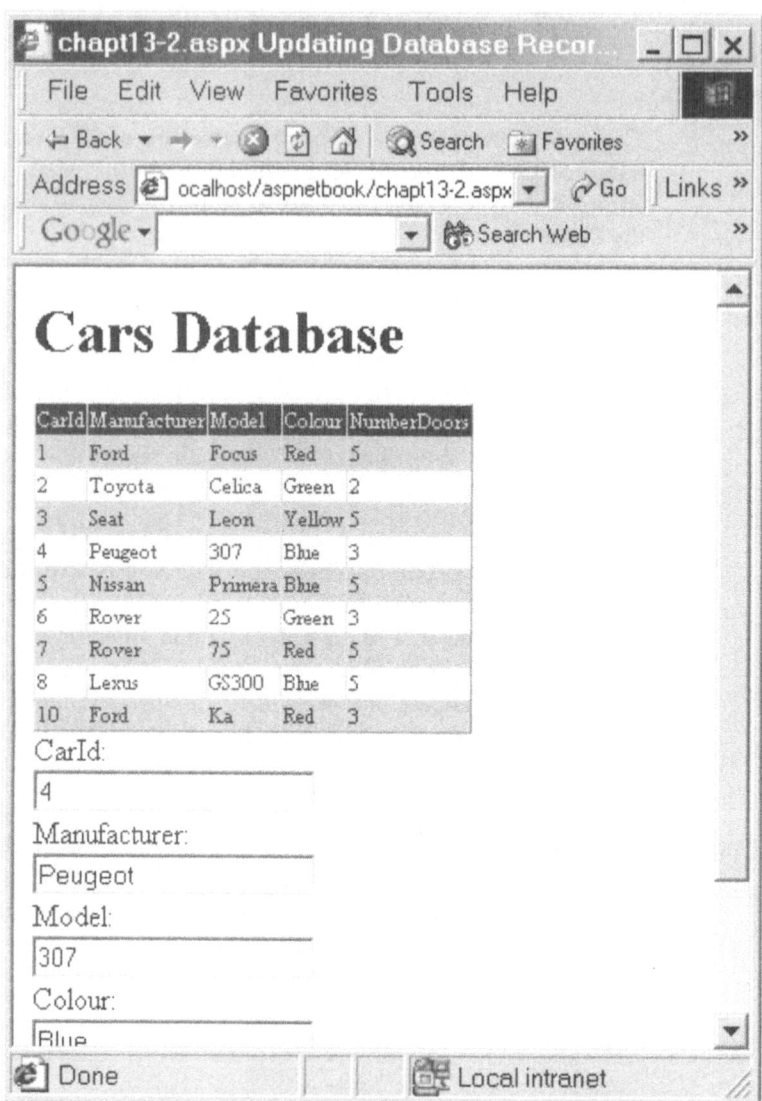

Figure 13.2 Updating records

Figure 13.2 illustrates that database record 4 has been updated. It now contains a Model of 307 and a Colour of Blue, while previously it was a 206 and Silver.

Deleting Records

Deleting of database records is also similar to adding and amending records. The SQL syntax for deleting a record is:

```
myCommand = New OleDbCommand("DELETE From Cars WHERE
CarId='1'",myConnection)
```

The following script illustrates deleting database records:

```
<%@Page Explicit="True" Language="VB" Strict="True" Debug="True" %>
<%@Import Namespace="System.Data" %>
<%@Import namespace="System.Data.Oledb" %>
<html>
     <head>
     <title>chapt13-3.aspx Deleting Database Records</title>
     </head>

     <script runat="server">

          Sub Page_Load (Sender As Object, E As EventArgs)
               Dim strConnection As String =
"Provider=Microsoft.Jet.OLEDB.4.0;Data Source=c:\cars.mdb"
               Dim strCommand As String = "Select * From Cars"
               Dim myConnect As OleDbConnection = New OleDbConnection
               Dim myAdaptor As OleDbDataAdapter = New
OleDbDataAdapter
               Dim CarsDataSet As DataSet = New DataSet

               myConnect.ConnectionString = strConnection
               myAdaptor.SelectCommand = New
OleDbCommand(strCommand,myConnect)
               myAdaptor.SelectCommand.Connection.Open

               myAdaptor.Fill(CarsDataSet, "Cars")

               carsTable.DataSource = CarsDataSet.Tables("Cars")
```

```
                    carsTable.DataBind
            End Sub

        Sub DataGridDelete (Sender As Object, E As DataGridCommandEventArgs)
                Dim idColumn As TableCell = e.Item.Cells(0)
                Dim intCarId as Integer = CInt(idColumn.Text)
                Dim myConnection As OleDbConnection
                Dim myCommand As OleDbCommand


                myConnection = New
OleDbConnection("Provider=Microsoft.Jet.OLEDB.4.0;Data Source=c:\cars.mdb")
                myConnection.Open()

                myCommand = New OleDbCommand("DELETE From Cars WHERE
CarId=" & intCarId,myConnection)

                myCommand.ExecuteNonQuery()
                myConnection.Close()
            End Sub

    </script>

    <body>
    <h1>Cars Database</h1>
    <form runat="server">
    <asp:datagrid id="carsTable" runat="server"
        AutoGenerateColumns="False"
        OnItemCommand="DataGridDelete">

    <HeaderStyle BackColor="blue" ForeColor="yellow" Font-Size="8pt" />
    <ItemStyle BackColor="lightgreen" ForeColor="blue" Font-Size="8pt" />
    <AlternatingItemStyle BackColor="white" ForeColor="blue" Font-Size="8pt" />

    <Columns>
            <asp:BoundColumn DataField="CarId" HeaderText="CarId" />
            <asp:BoundColumn DataField="Make" HeaderText="Manufacturer" />
            <asp:BoundColumn DataField="Model" HeaderText="Model" />
            <asp:BoundColumn DataField="Colour" HeaderText="Colour" />

            <asp:BoundColumn DataField="NumberDoors"
HeaderText="NumberDoors" />
```

```
        <asp:ButtonColumn Text="Delete" HeaderText="Delete" />

    </Columns>
    </asp:datagrid>
    </form>
    </body>
</html>
```

The output from the above script is illustrates in Figure 13.3.

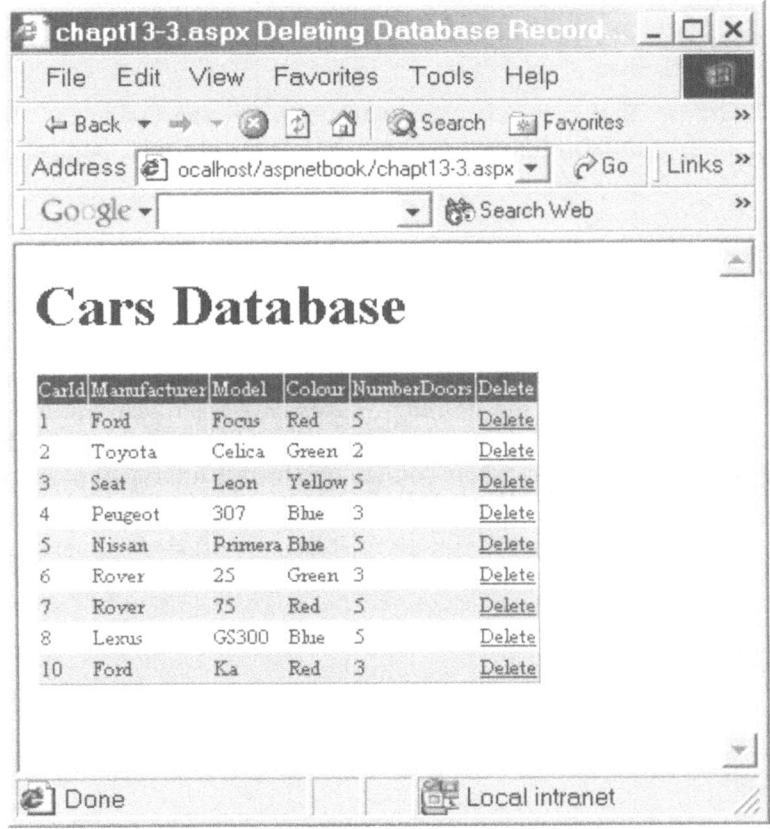

Figure 13.3 Deleting records

The above script differs somewhat from the previous two examples in this chapter as it just uses the DataGrid control to both display all records and to allow the user to select which record to delete. The script uses the DataGrid ButtonColumn control to invoke the DataGridDelete subroutine:

```
<asp:ButtonColumn Text="Delete" HeaderText="Delete" />
```

This subroutine determines which record to delete by accessing the CarId passed by the ButtonColumn control:

```
myCommand = New OleDbCommand("DELETE From Cars WHERE CarId=" &
intCarId,myConnection)
```

The rest of the subroutine is the same as the DataGridUpdate subroutine from the previous example.

Summary

In this chapter we have examined how databases can be interacted with from a web page. Examples of adding, updating and deleting records have been included. In the following and final chapter we shall provide some useful suggestions where you can find further information.

Chapter 14

Where Next?

Introduction

No book, certainly not one of this length, can provide you will all the information you will need as your knowledge of ASP.NET grows. However, the Web is a great resource of information and in this chapter a number of the best resources available are described.

Microsoft ASP.NET

Microsoft house the official ASP.NET site and it is very good indeed. In fact if you type ASP.NET into Google then this is the only page that is displayed! From here you can download the latest versions of the .NET framework, view and run code examples, find information of ASP.NET web hosting companies and so much more. You should make a point of visiting this site frequently to check up on news and updates.

http://www.asp.net/

4GuysFromRolla

A strange name but an excellent web site. Many example tutorials and articles on basic to advanced topics. A highly recommended site.

http://www.4guysfromrolla.com/

ASP Alliance

ASP Alliance claim to provide the number one ASP.NET Developer Community. Certainly their site contains good articles, tutorials and code examples.

http://www.aspalliance.com/

Brinkster

The Brinkster CodeBank is a code-sharing tool for the web development community. The purpose of the CodeBank is to allow developers to share and find Code Snippets they may need.

http://www.brinkster.com/

411 ASP.NET Directory

http://www.411asp.net/

LearnASP

A site run by Charles Carroll consisting of tutorials on ASP.NET, book reviews and code examples.

http://www.learnasp.com/learnasp/

DotNetJunkies

The DotNetJunkies Tutorial Index lists DotNetJunkies tutorials by topic to help you find the tutorial that suits your needs.

http://www.aspnextgen.com/tutorialsindex.aspx

And Finally ...

The ASP.NET community is vast and growing daily. There are many very knowledgeable developers out there who are only too pleased to help solve whatever ASP.NET problem you may have. Just don't be afraid to ask!

Index